I0462179

Real World

Colouring Book

For Advanced Users & Adults

50 Images

Created From Real Life Photos
For You To Colour As You Please.

ISBN 978-0-359-82301-7
90000
9 780359 823017

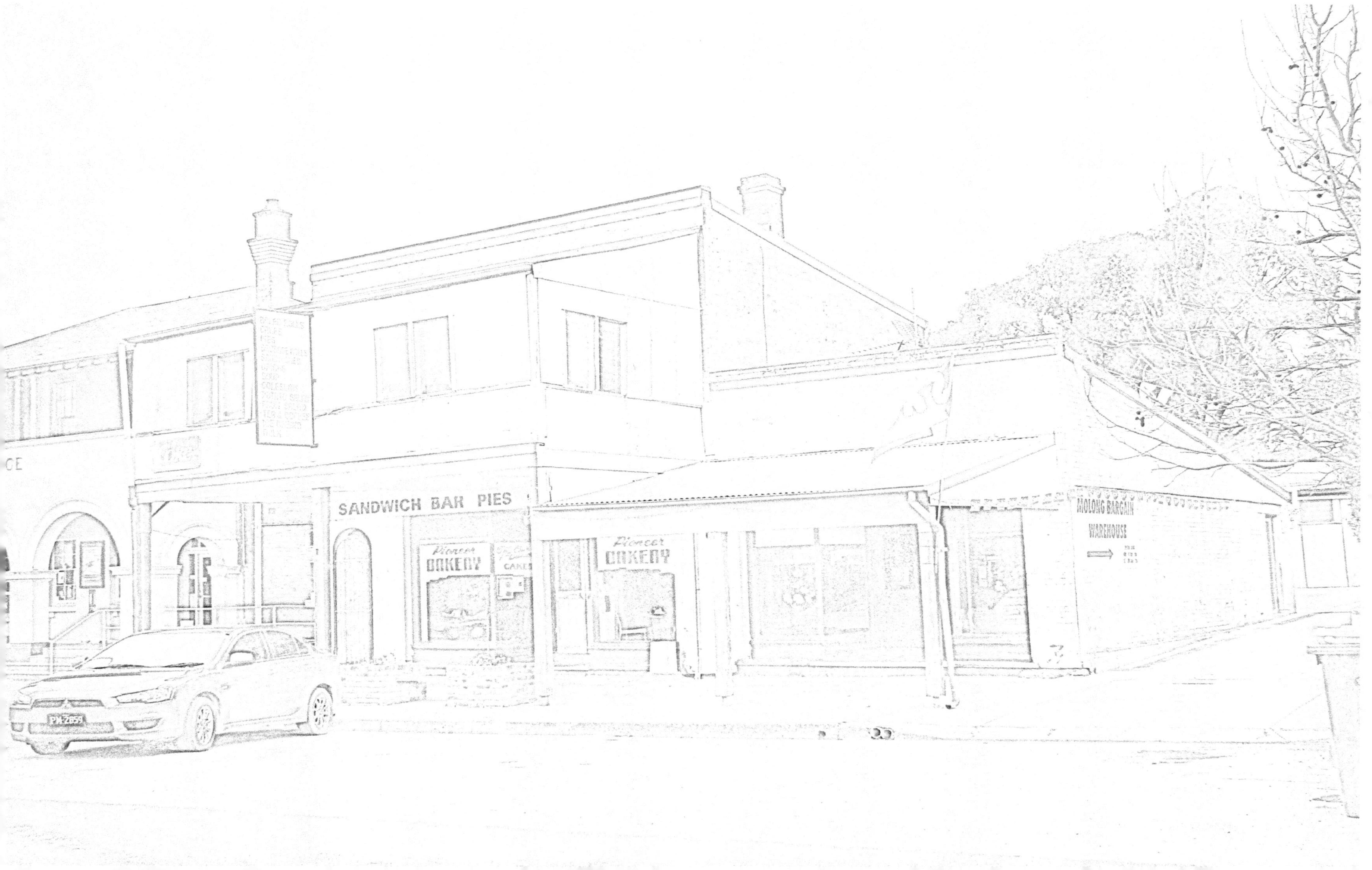
SANDWICH BAR PIES
Pioneer
BAKERY
CAKES
Pioneer
BAKERY
MOLONG BARGAIN
WAREHOUSE
PM-Z65S

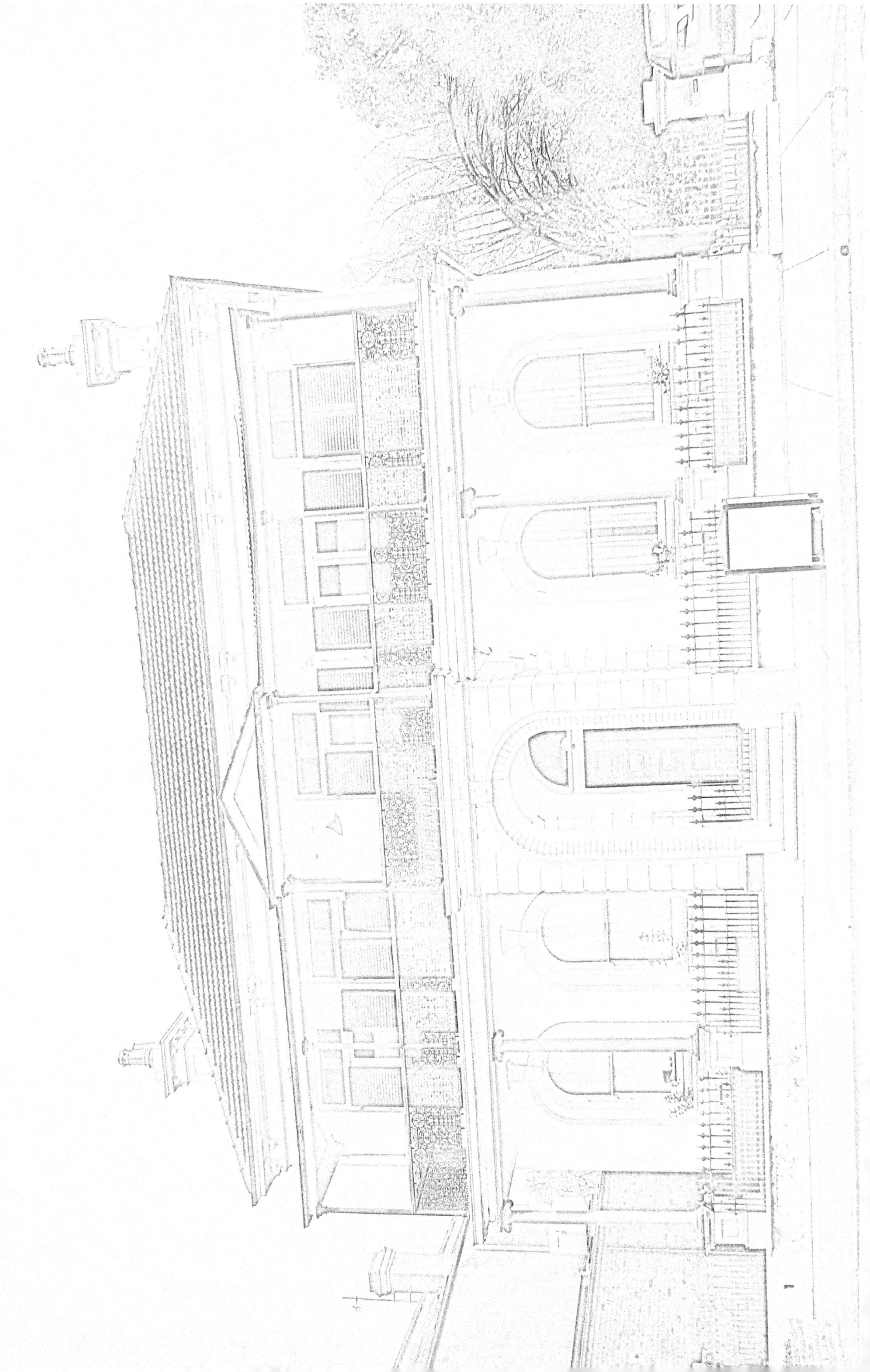

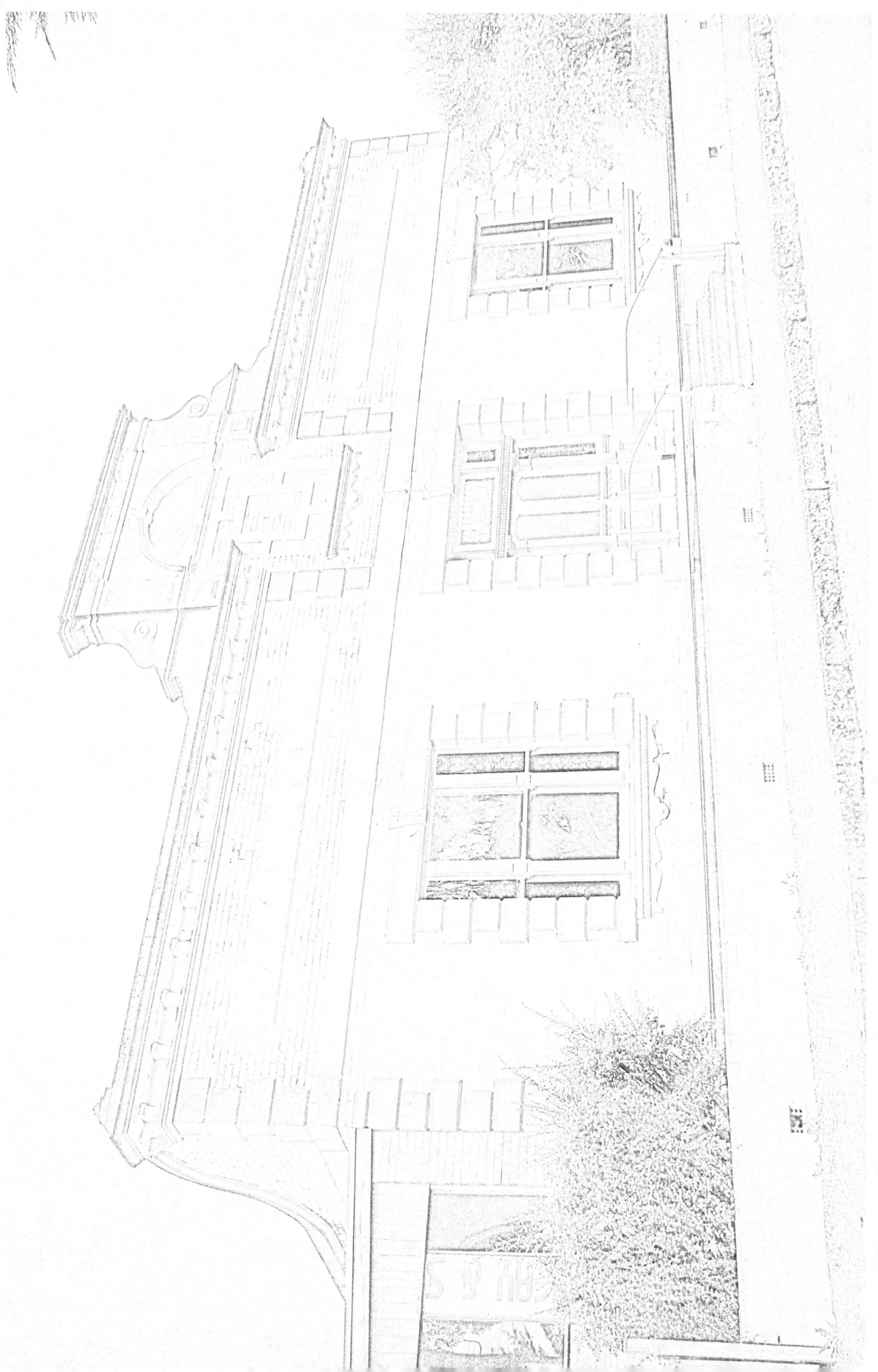

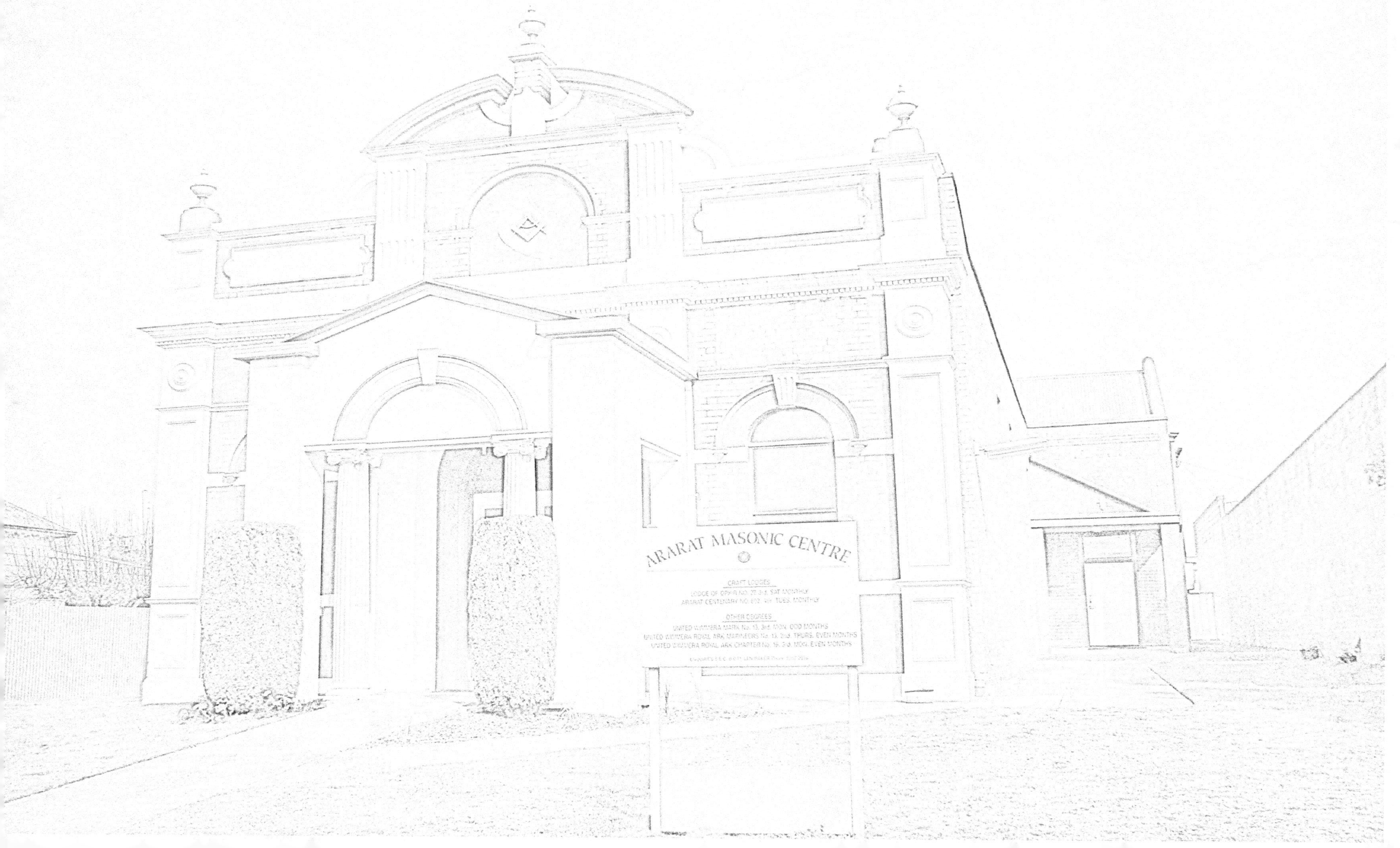
ARARAT MASONIC CENTRE
CRAFT LODGES
OTHER DEGREES

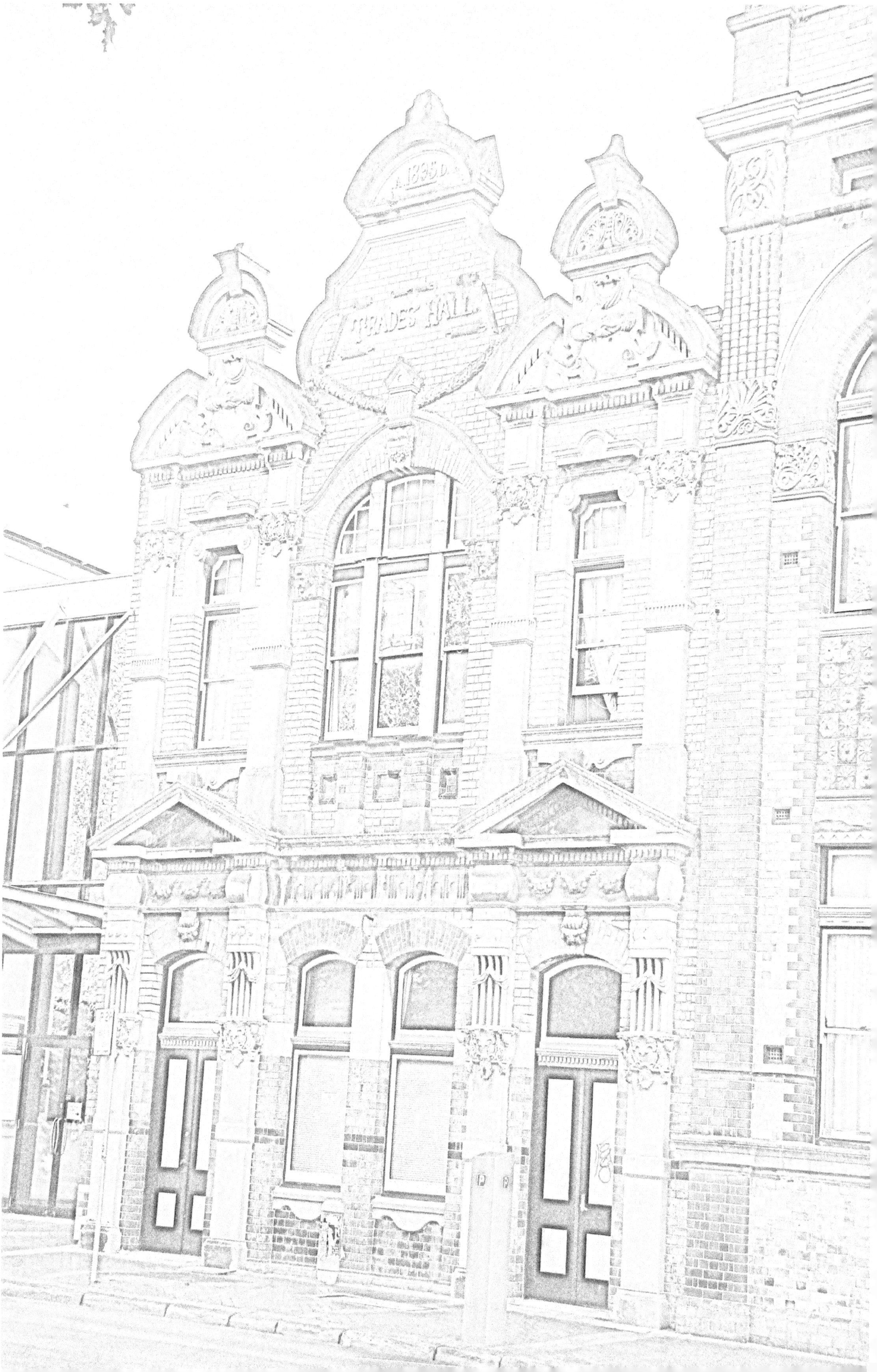
TRADES' HALL

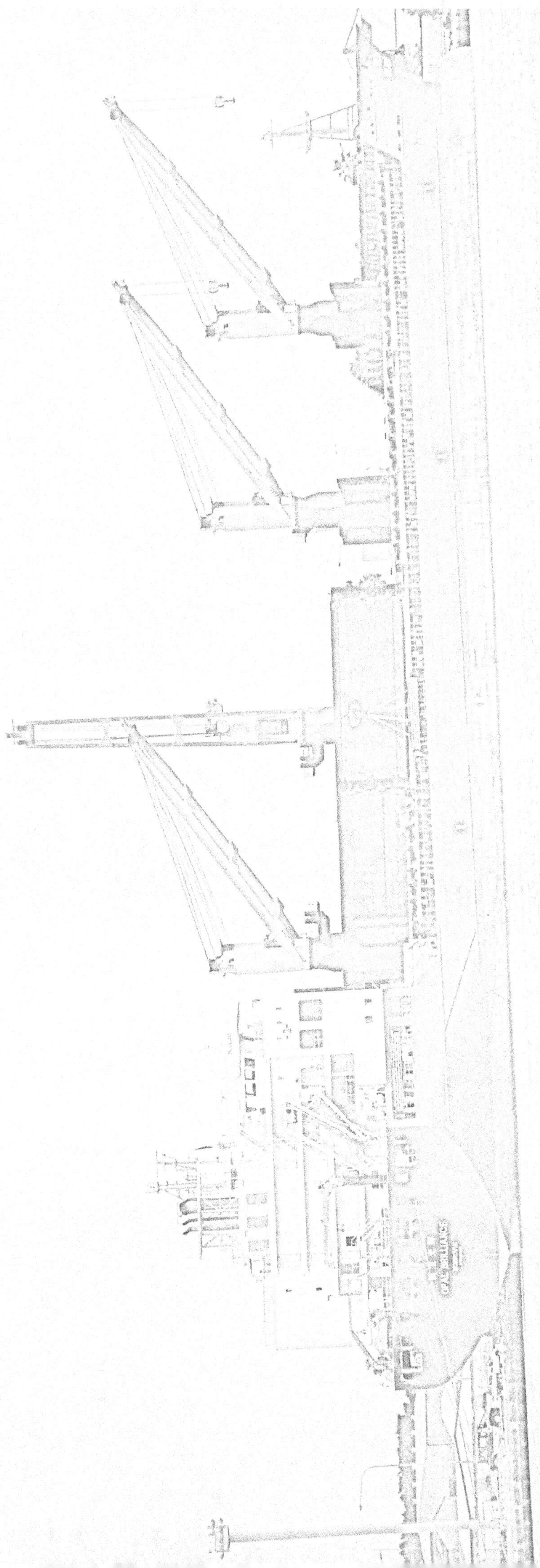

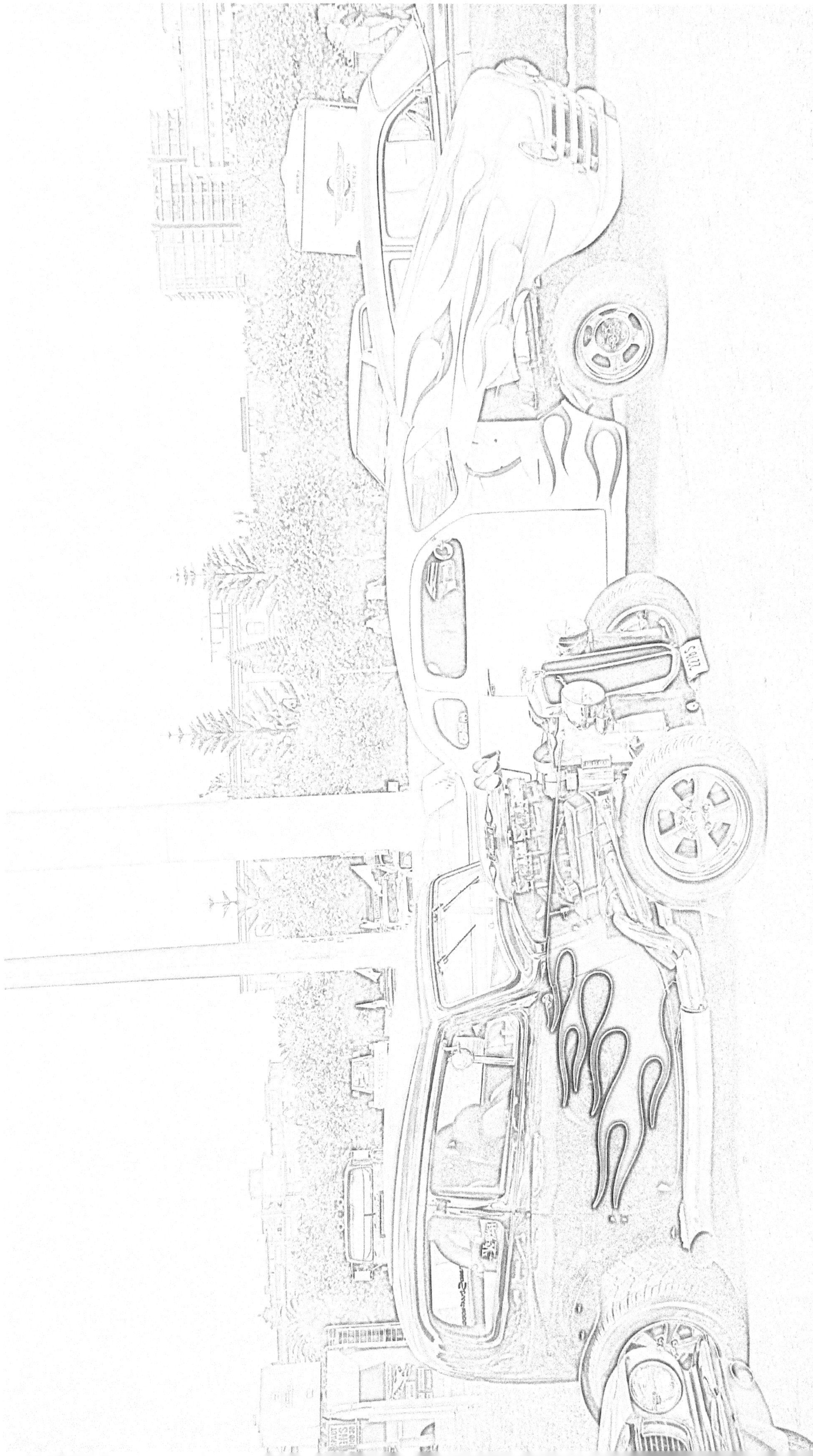

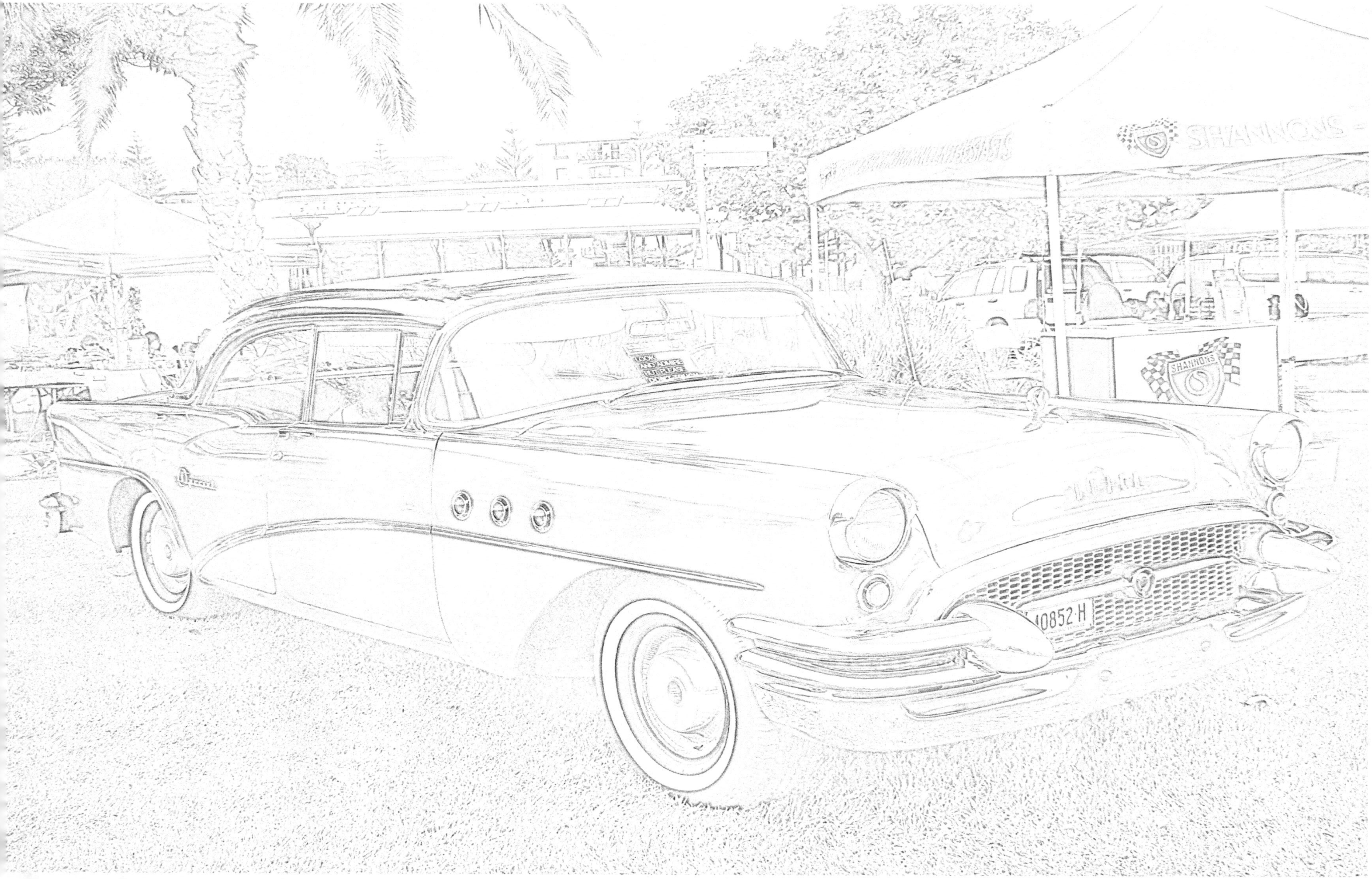
SHANNONS
SHANNONS
40852·H

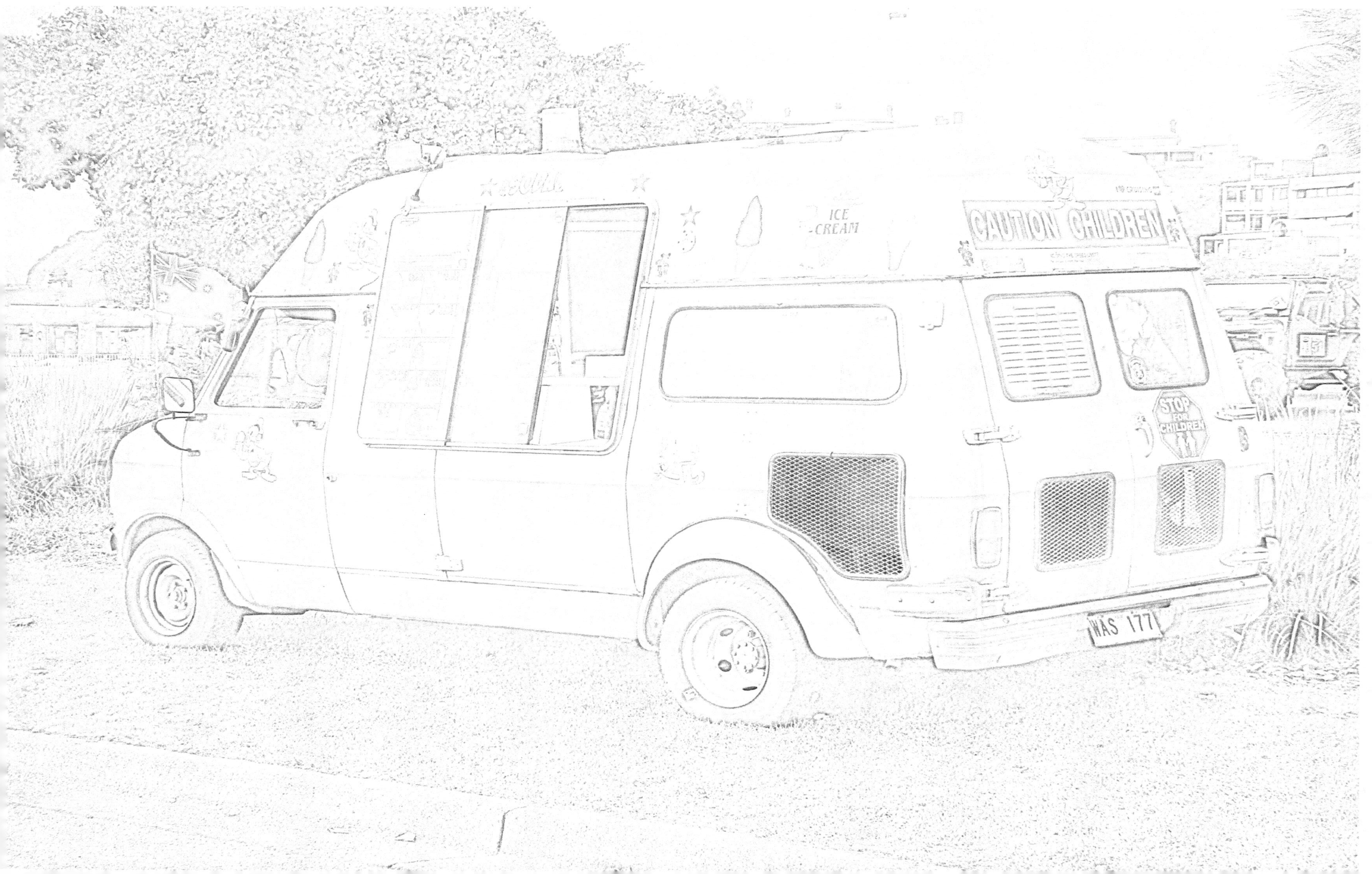
ICE
CREAM
CAUTION CHILDREN
STOP
FOR
CHILDREN
WAS 177

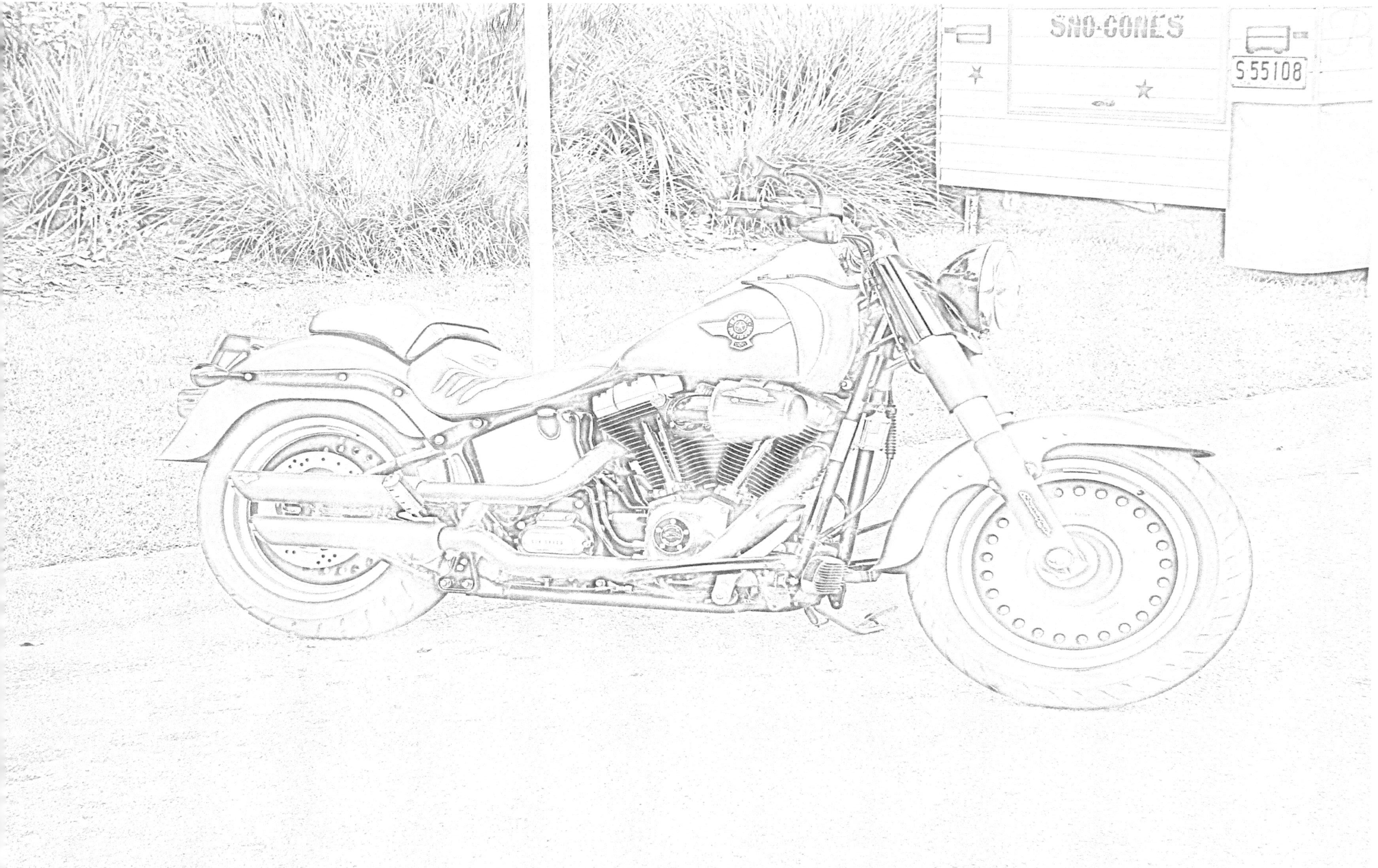
SNO-CONES
S 55108

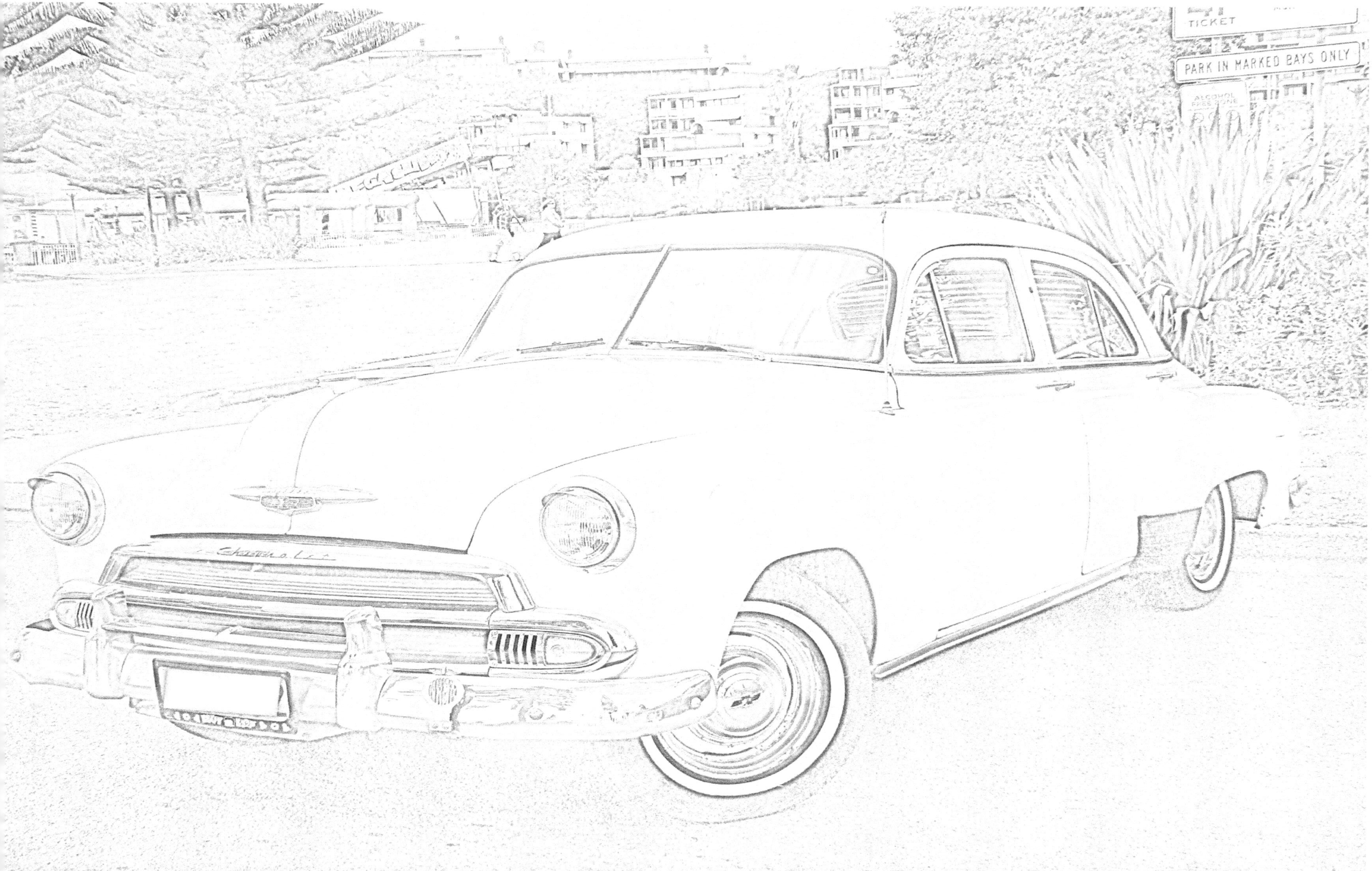
TICKET
PARK IN MARKED BAYS ONLY

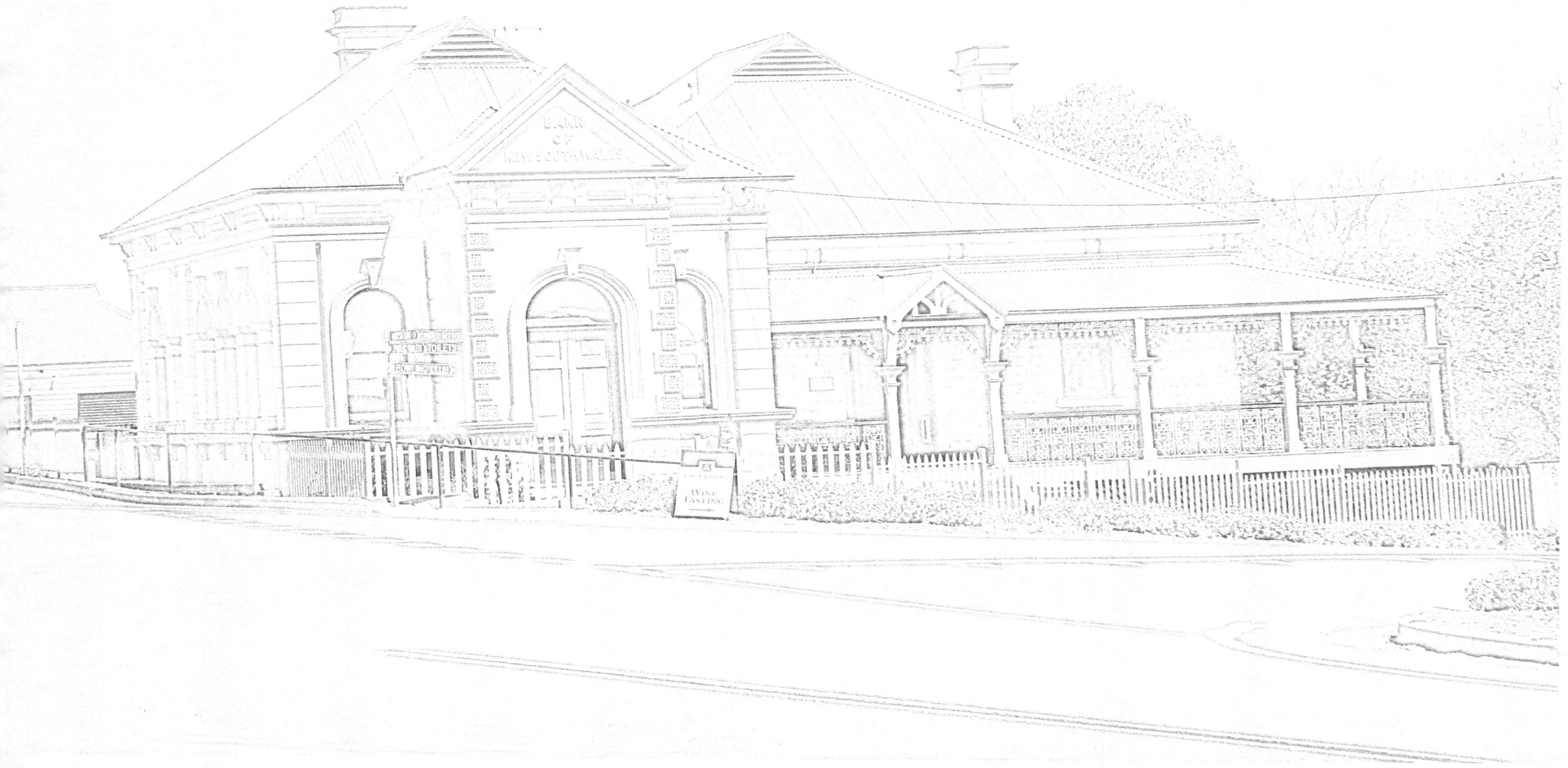
BANK
OF
NEW SOUTH WALES
BOWLING CLUB
WINE TASTING

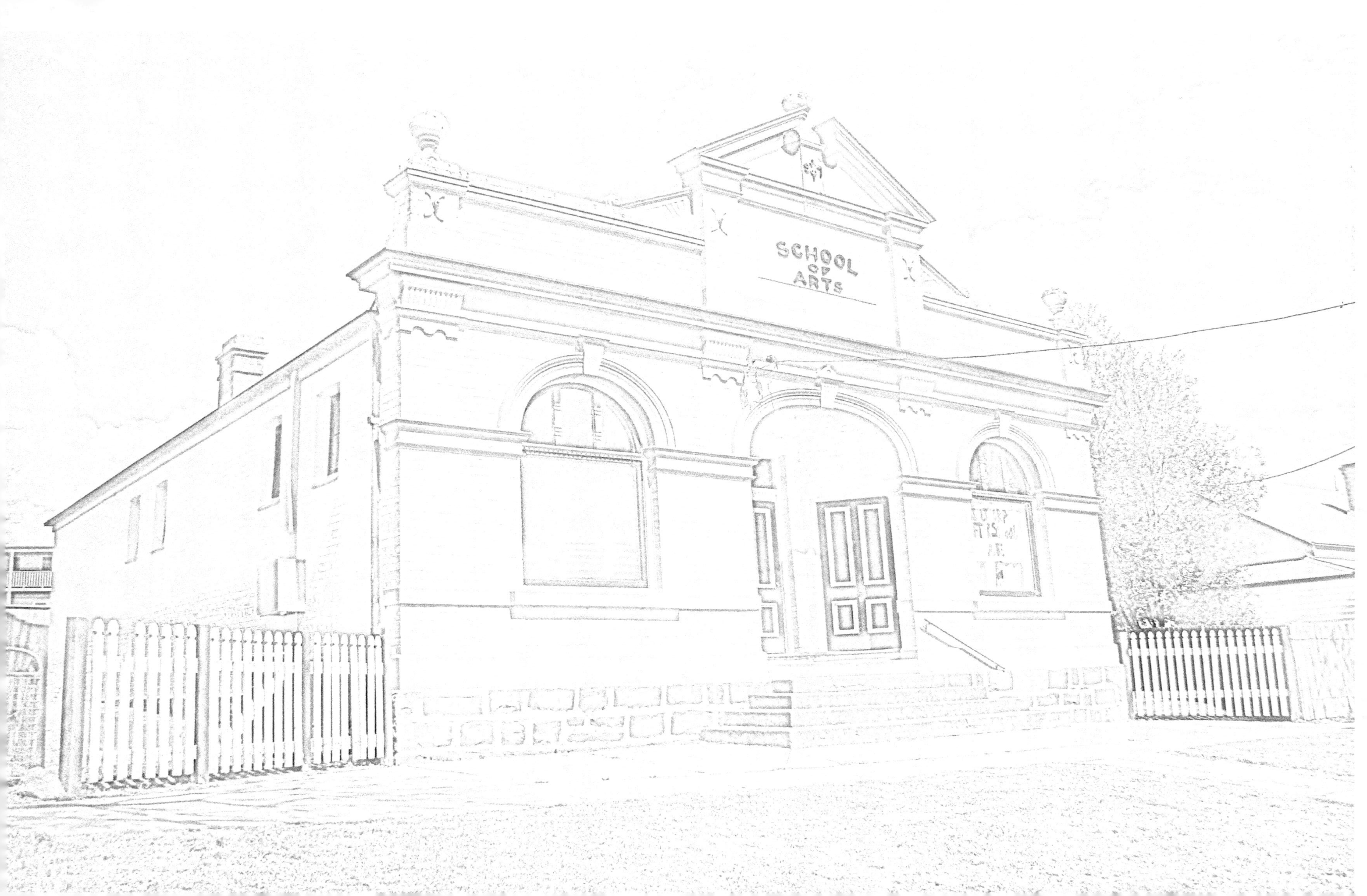
SCHOOL OF ARTS

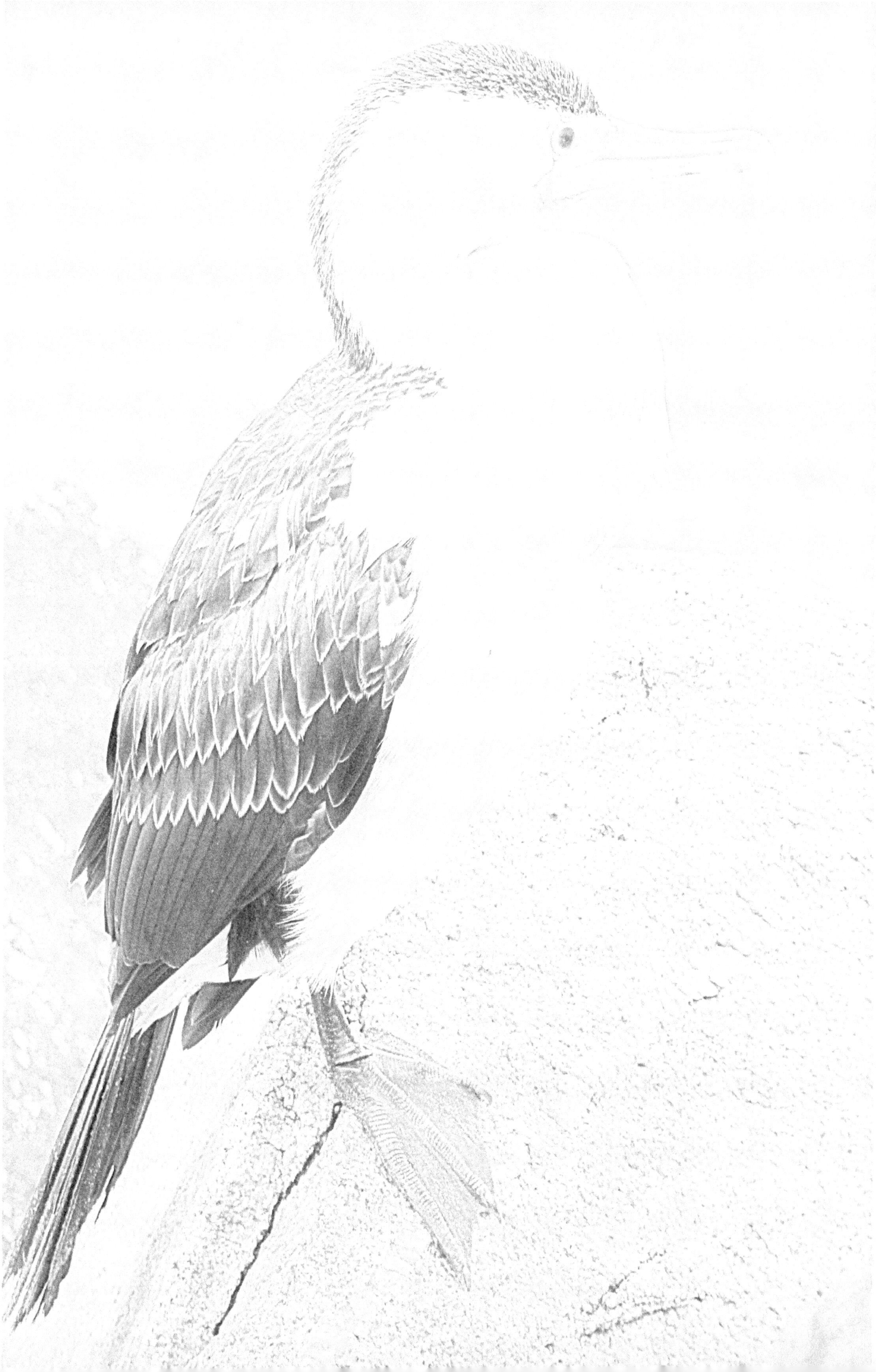

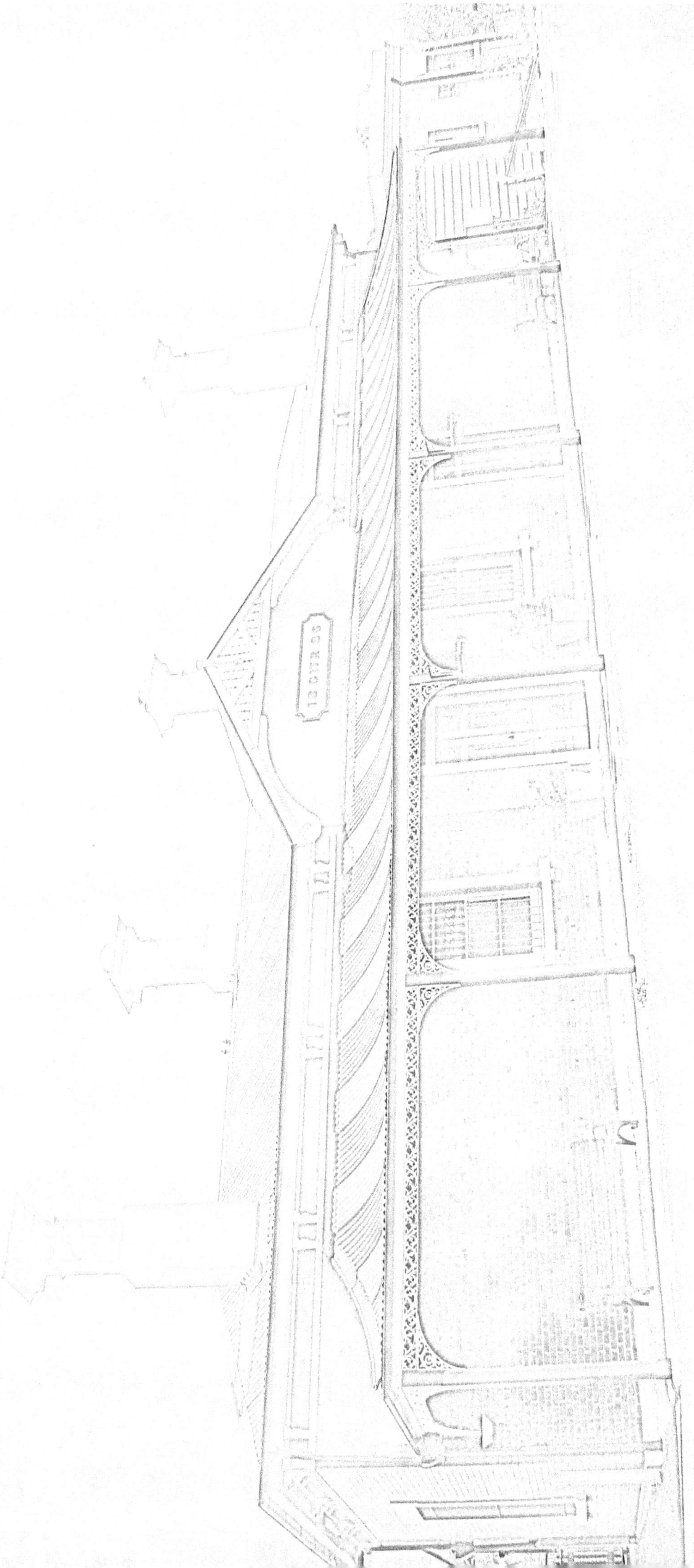

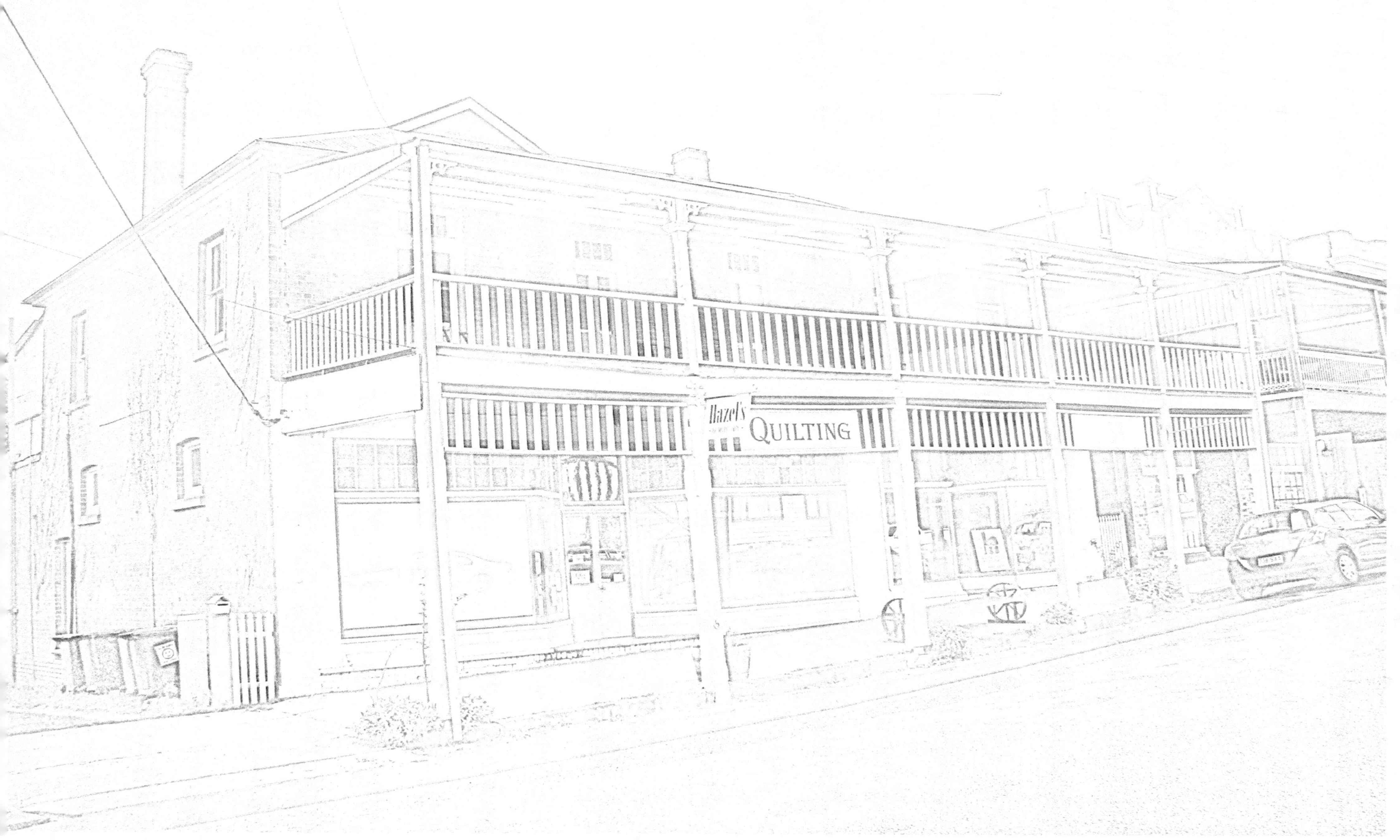
Hazel's
QUILTING

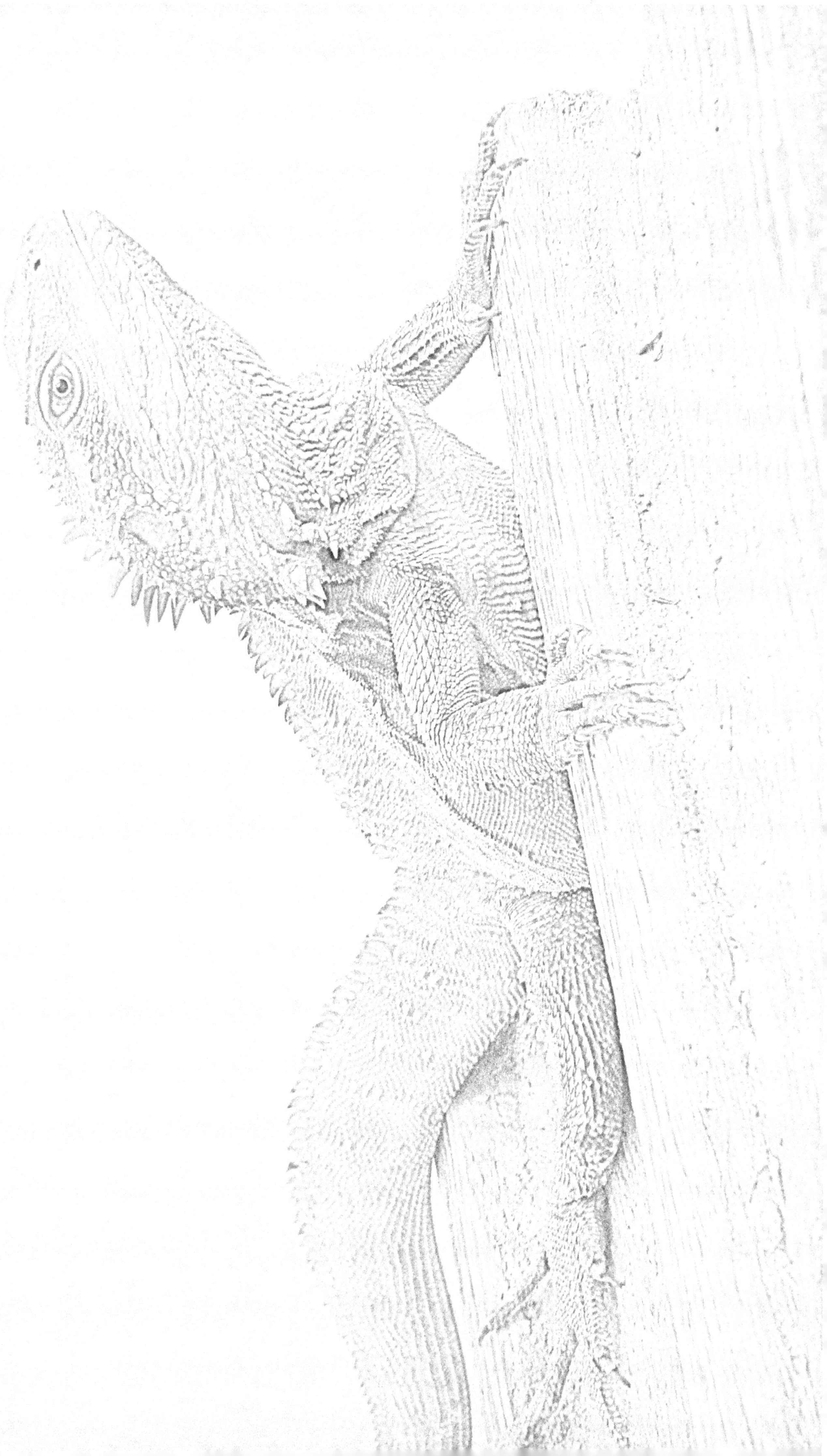

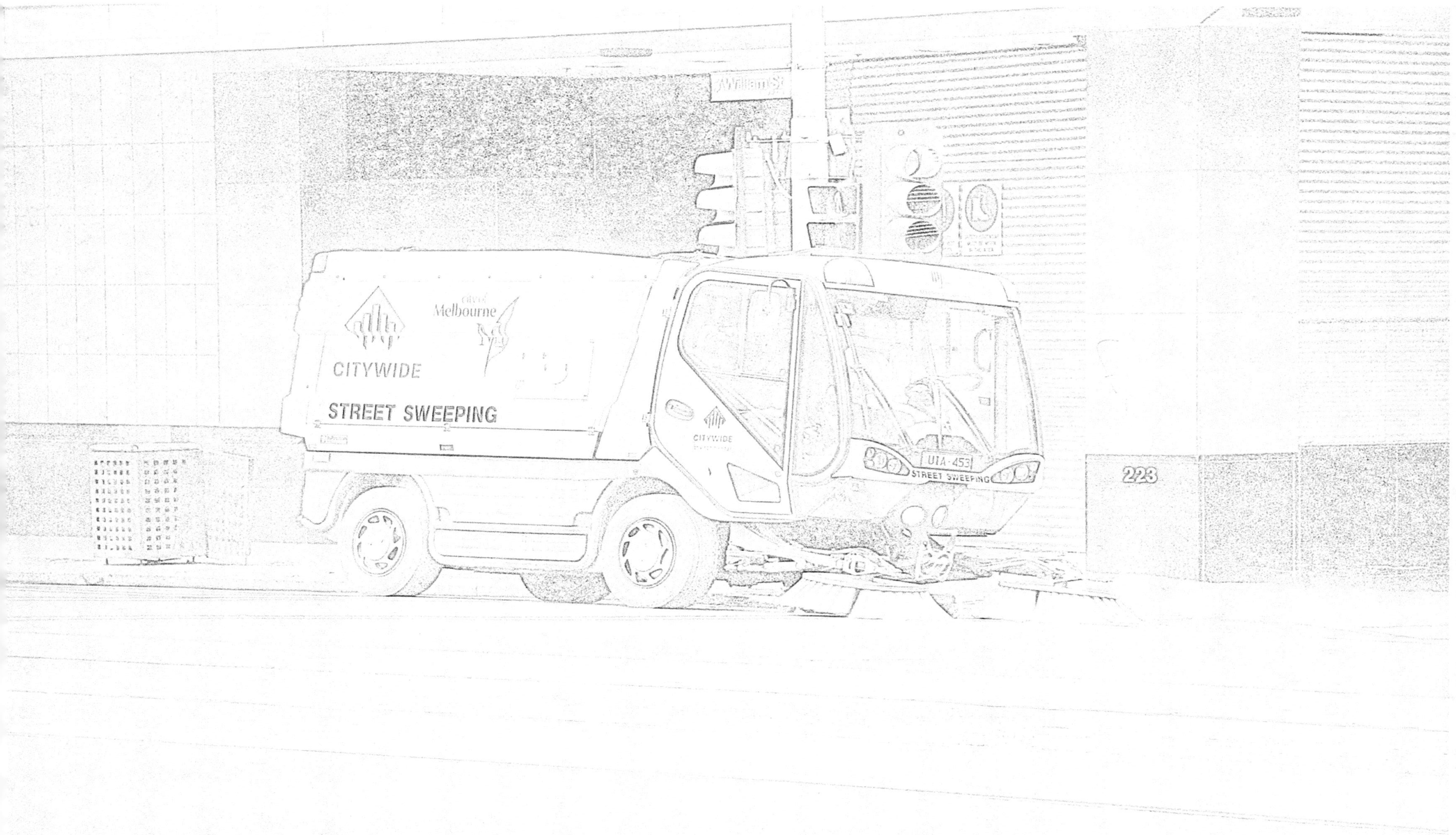
William St
CITYWIDE
STREET SWEEPING
city of Melbourne
CITYWIDE
UIA 453
STREET SWEEPING
223

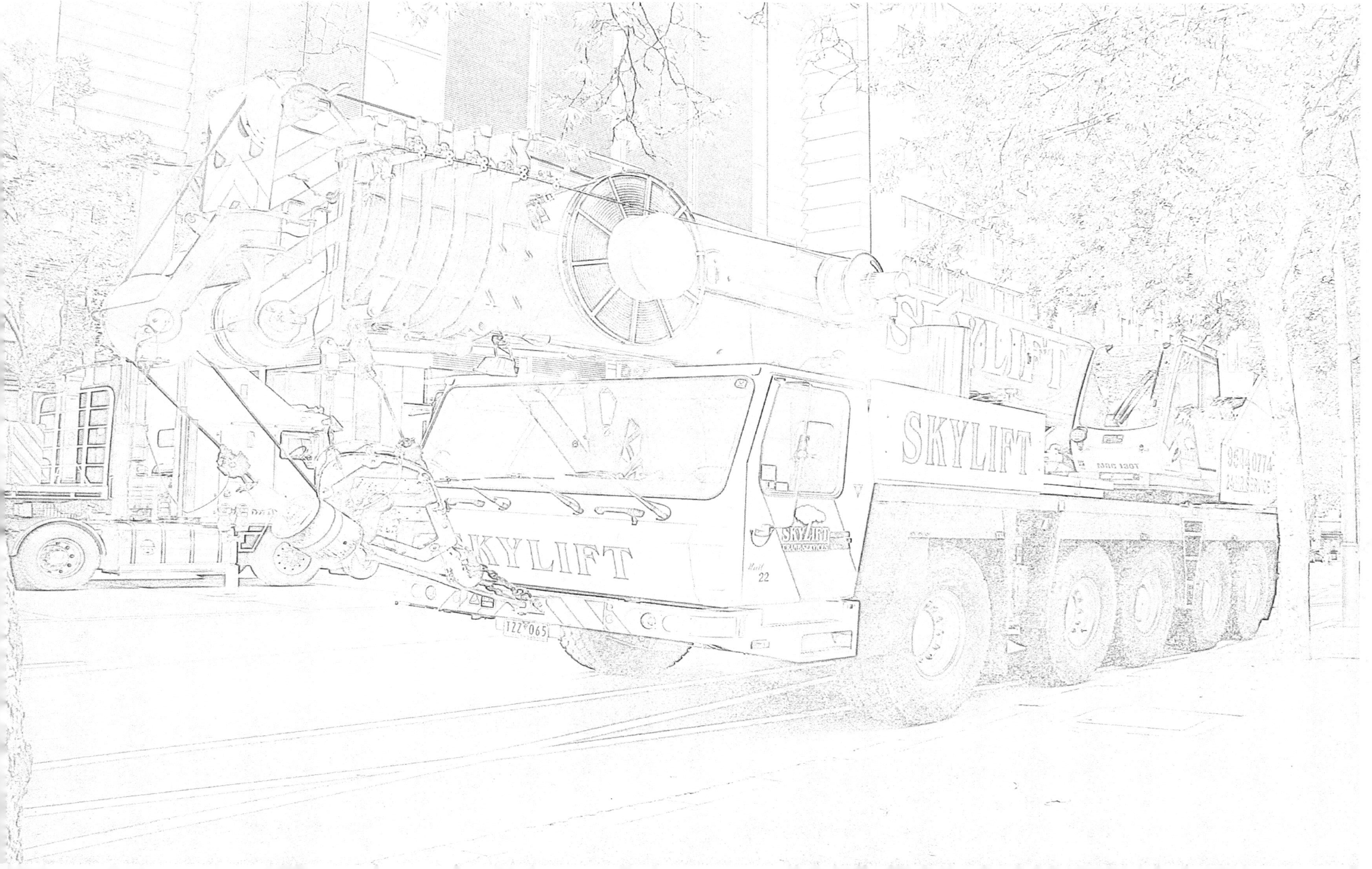
SKYLIFT
SKYLIFT
22
TZZ 065

BERNARDS
MAGIC SHOP
BERNARDS
MAGIC SHOP
Est. 1937
209
SEIKO
209 REPAIR CENTRE
Thomas Sabo
CLOSE
Breakfast Lunch Sa
Lunch Coffee
Coffee Smoothies

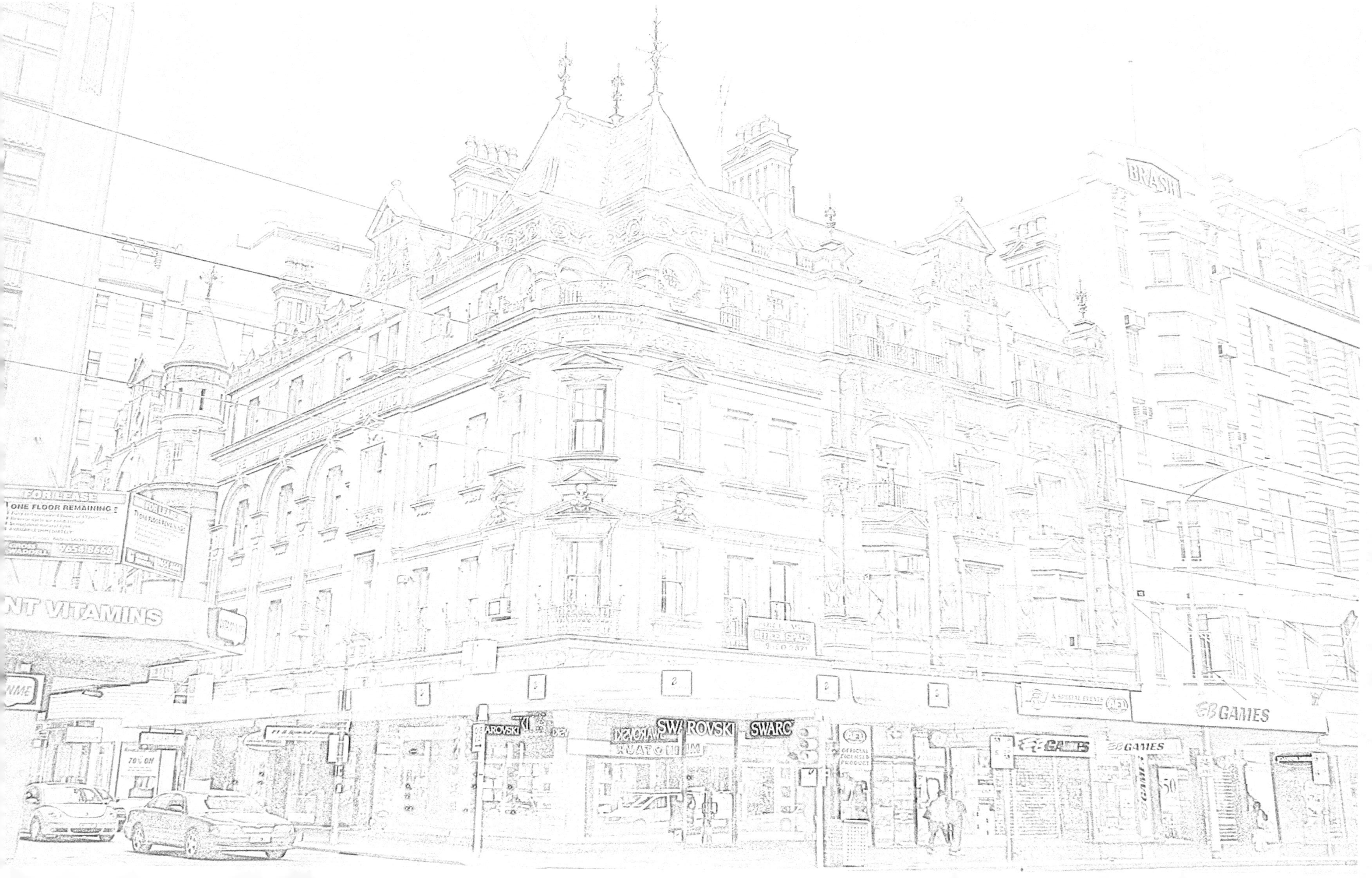
FOR LEASE
ONE FLOOR REMAINING
NT VITAMINS
BRASH
SWAROVSKI
SWARC
EB GAMES
70% OFF

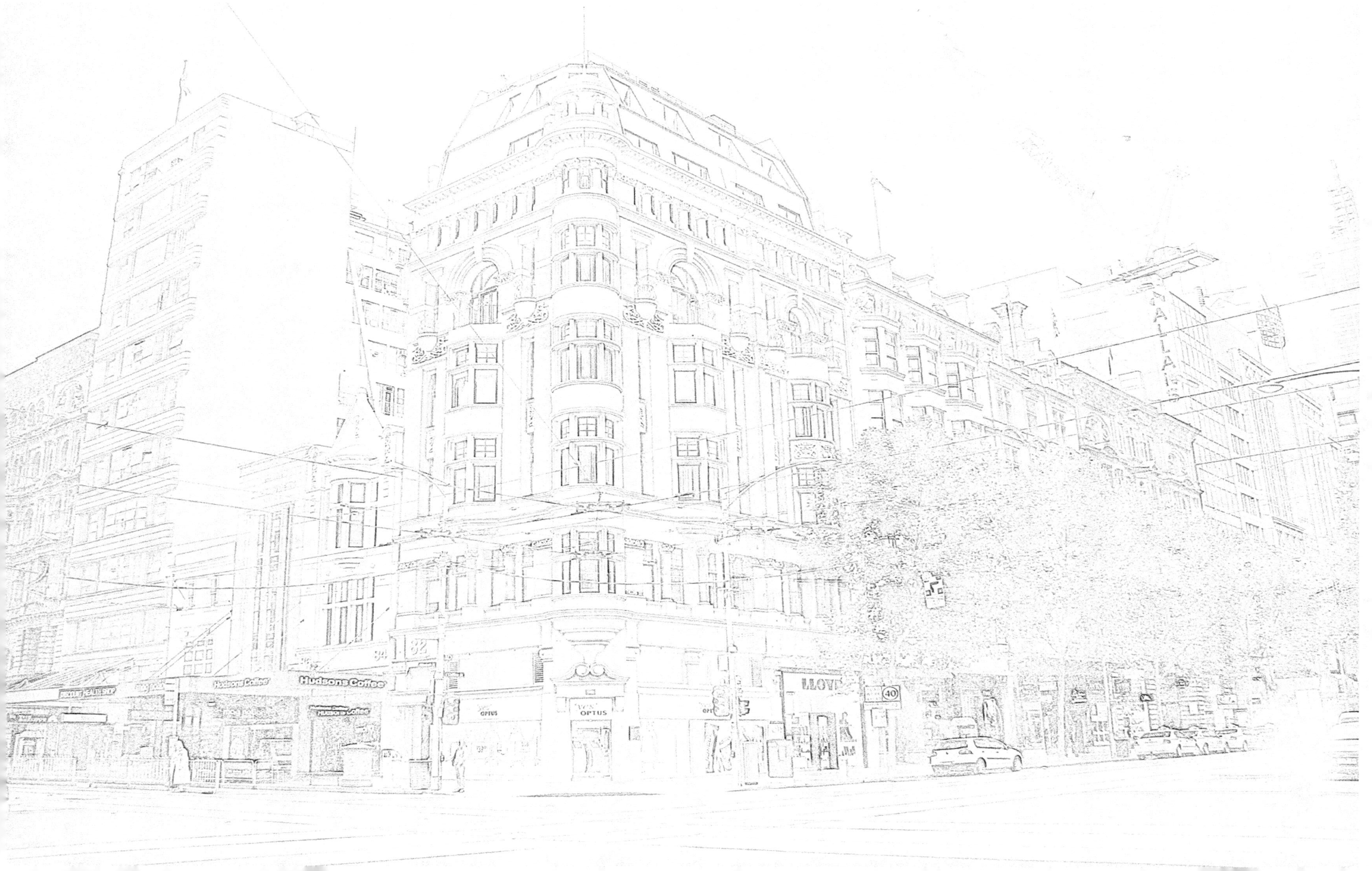
Hudsons Coffee
Hudsons Coffee
OPTUS
OPTUS
40
32

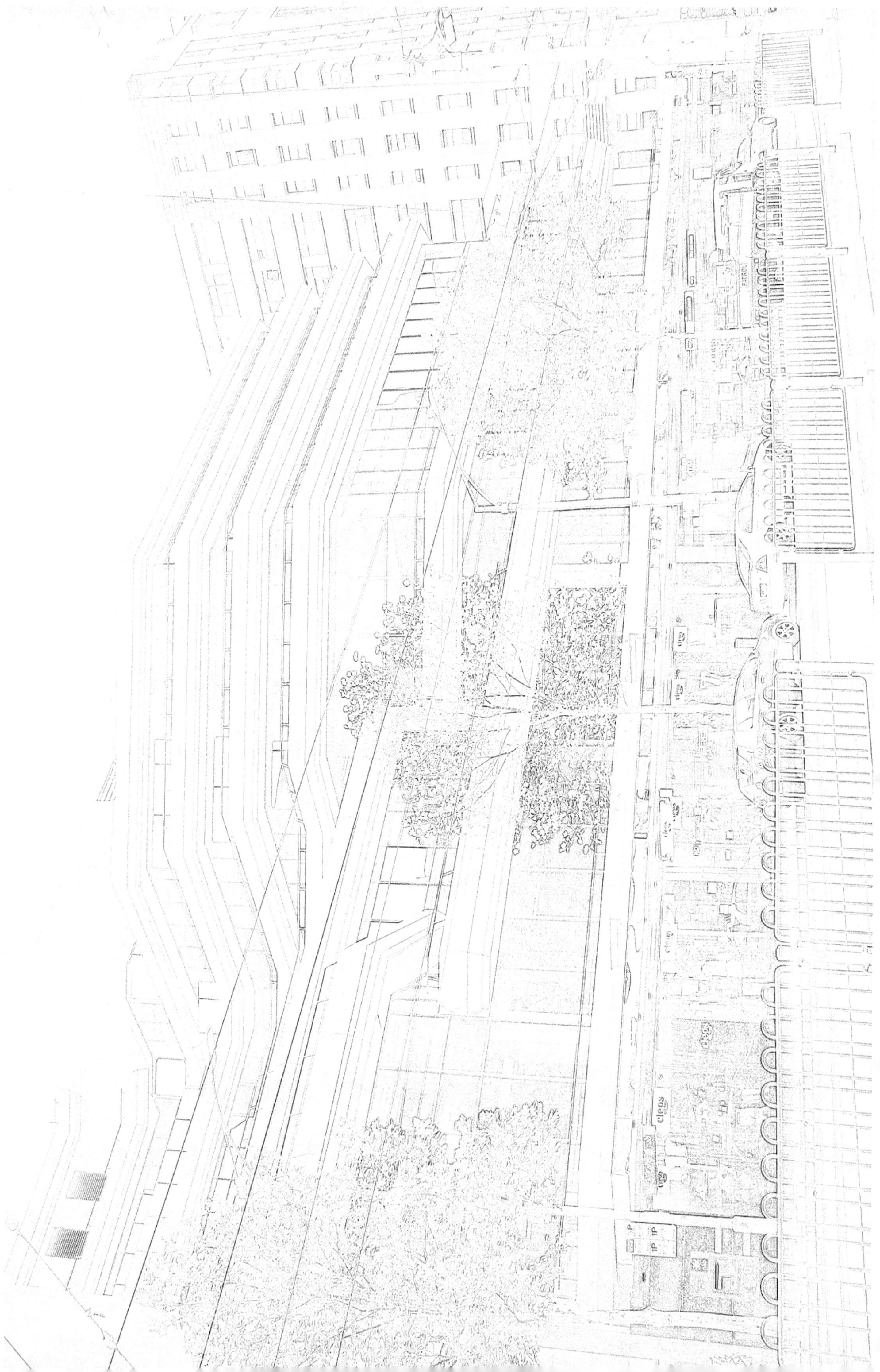
cleos
PETROL

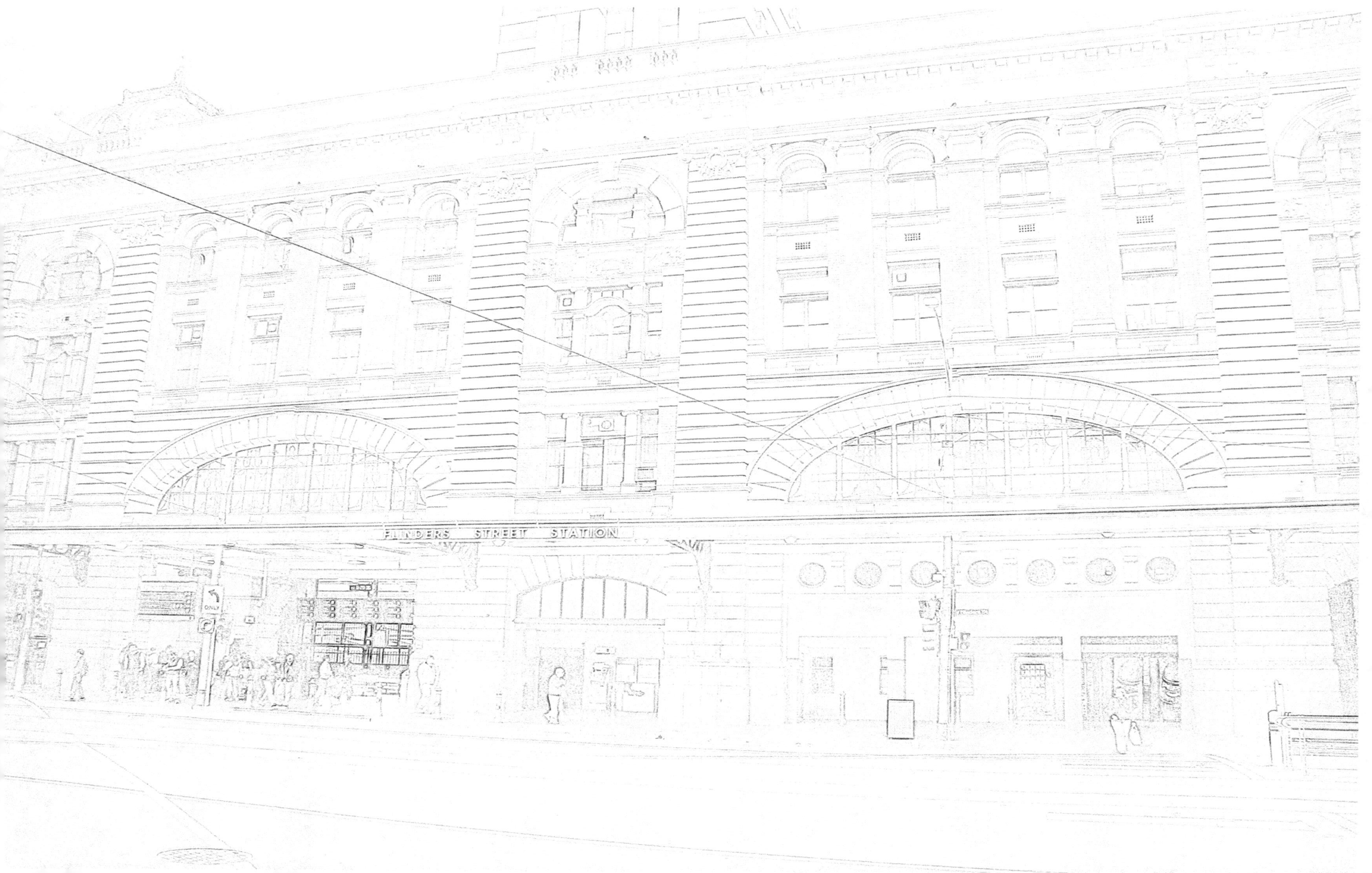
FLINDERS STREET STATION
ONLY

FLINDERS STREET STATION

melbourne food wine
Join In
FLINDERS STREET STATION
melbourne food wine
Join In

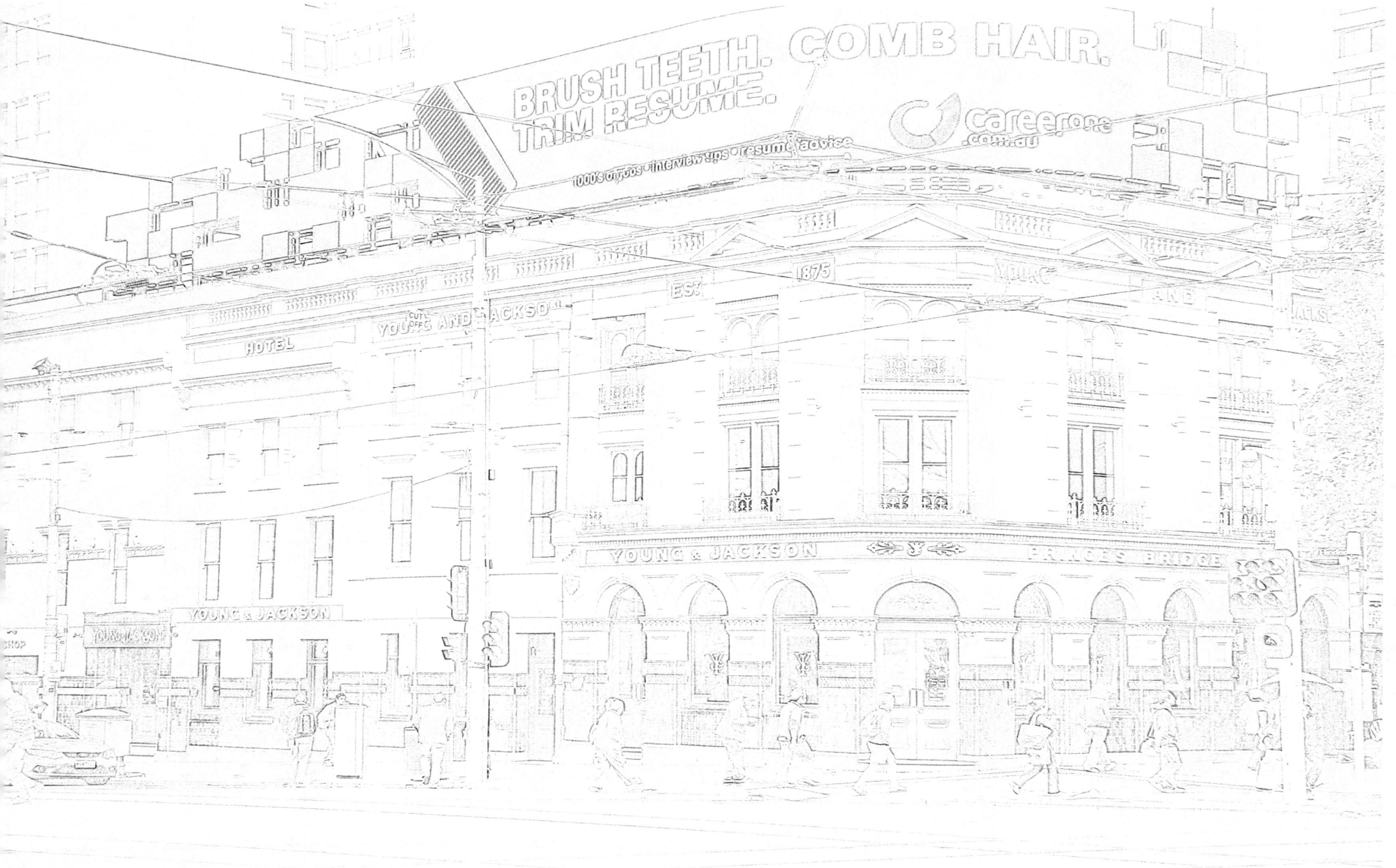
BRUSH TEETH. COMB HAIR.
TRIM RESUME.
careerone
.com.au
1000's of jobs • interview tips • resume advice
1875
EST
HOTEL
YOUNG AND JACKSON
YOUNG & JACKSON
PRINCES BRIDGE
YOUNG & JACKSON

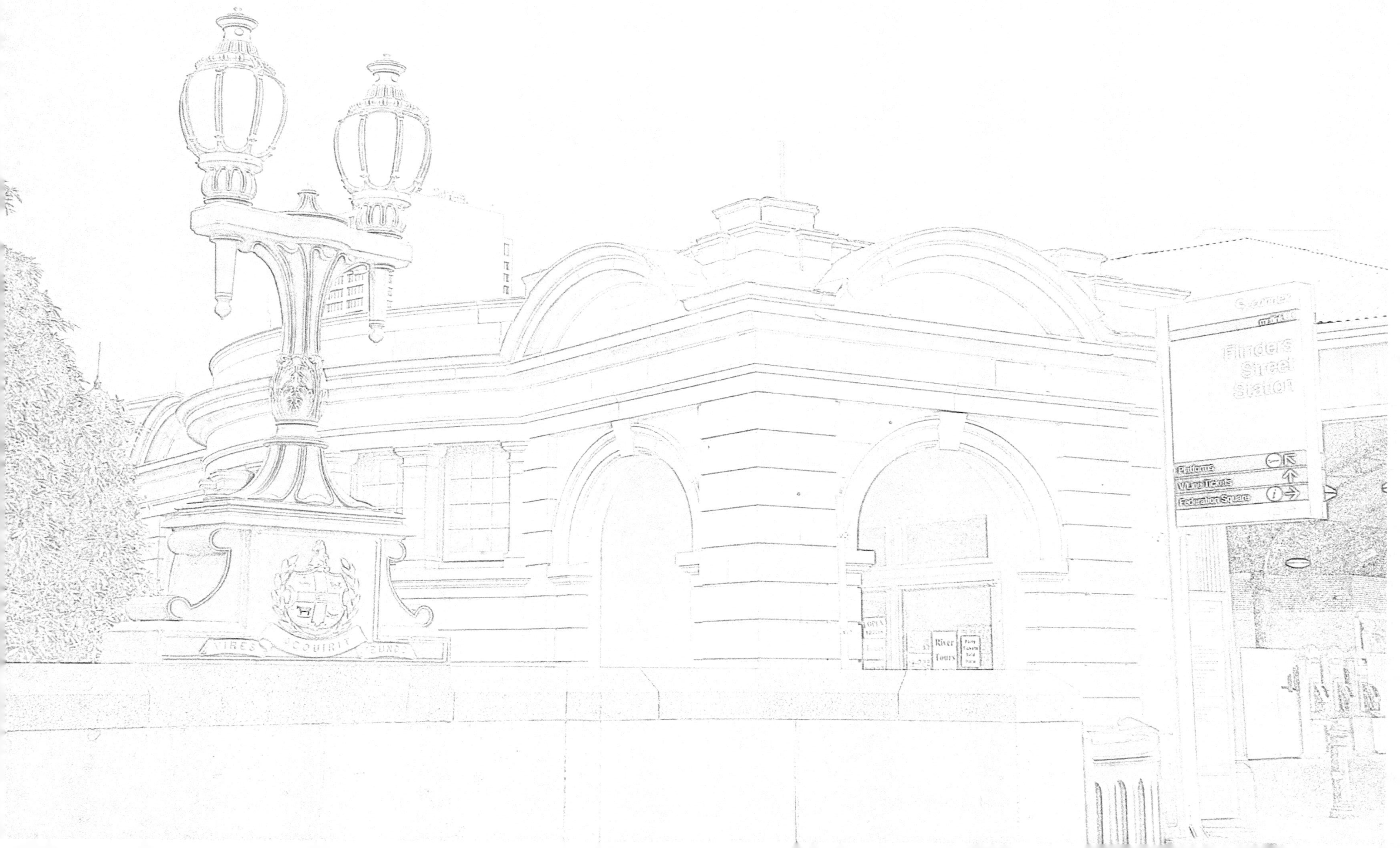

Flinders Street Station
Platforms
V/Line Tickets
Federation Square
River Tours
VIRES ACQUIRIT EUNDO

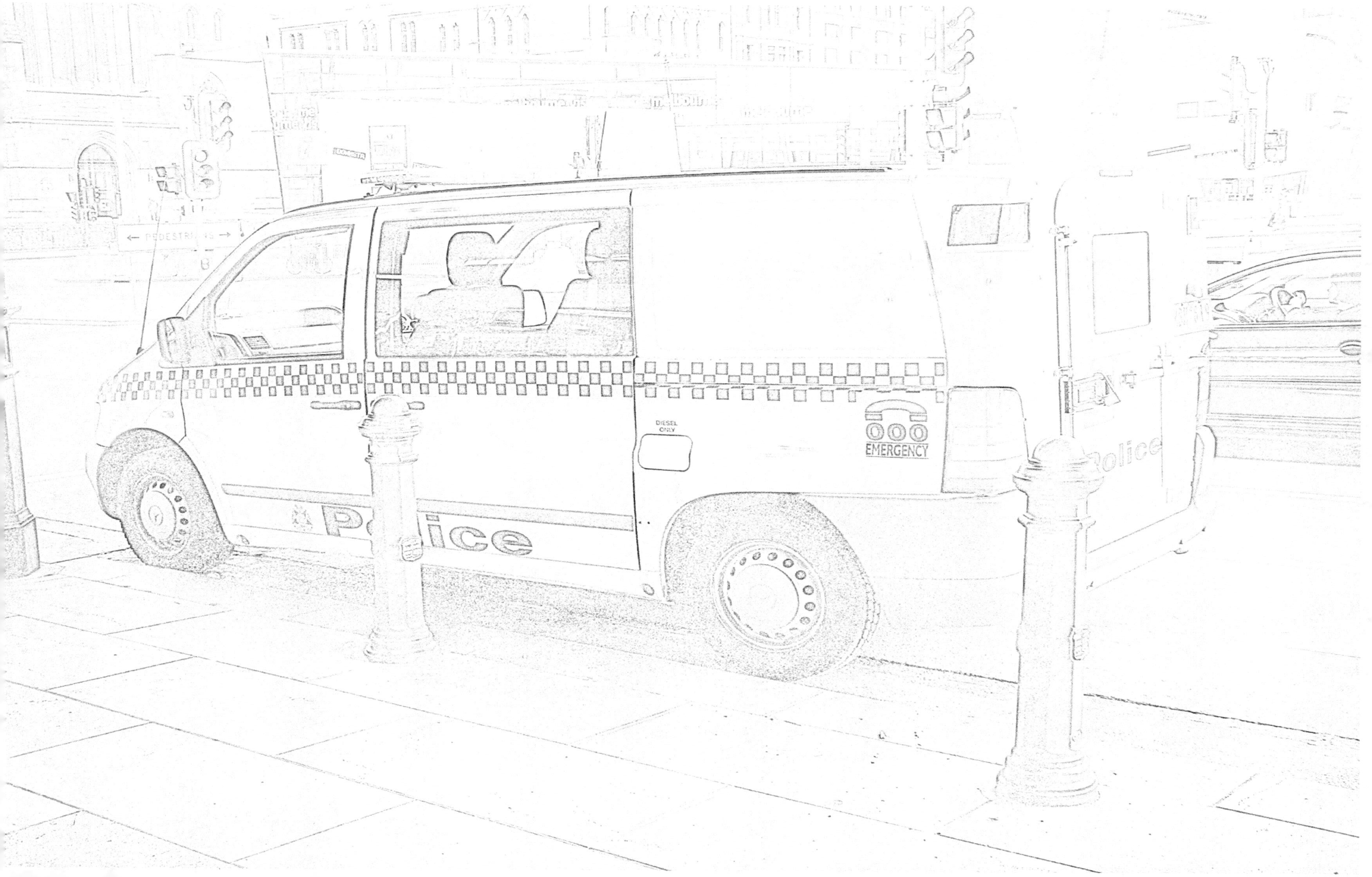

← PEDESTRIANS →
000
EMERGENCY
DIESEL ONLY
Police
Police

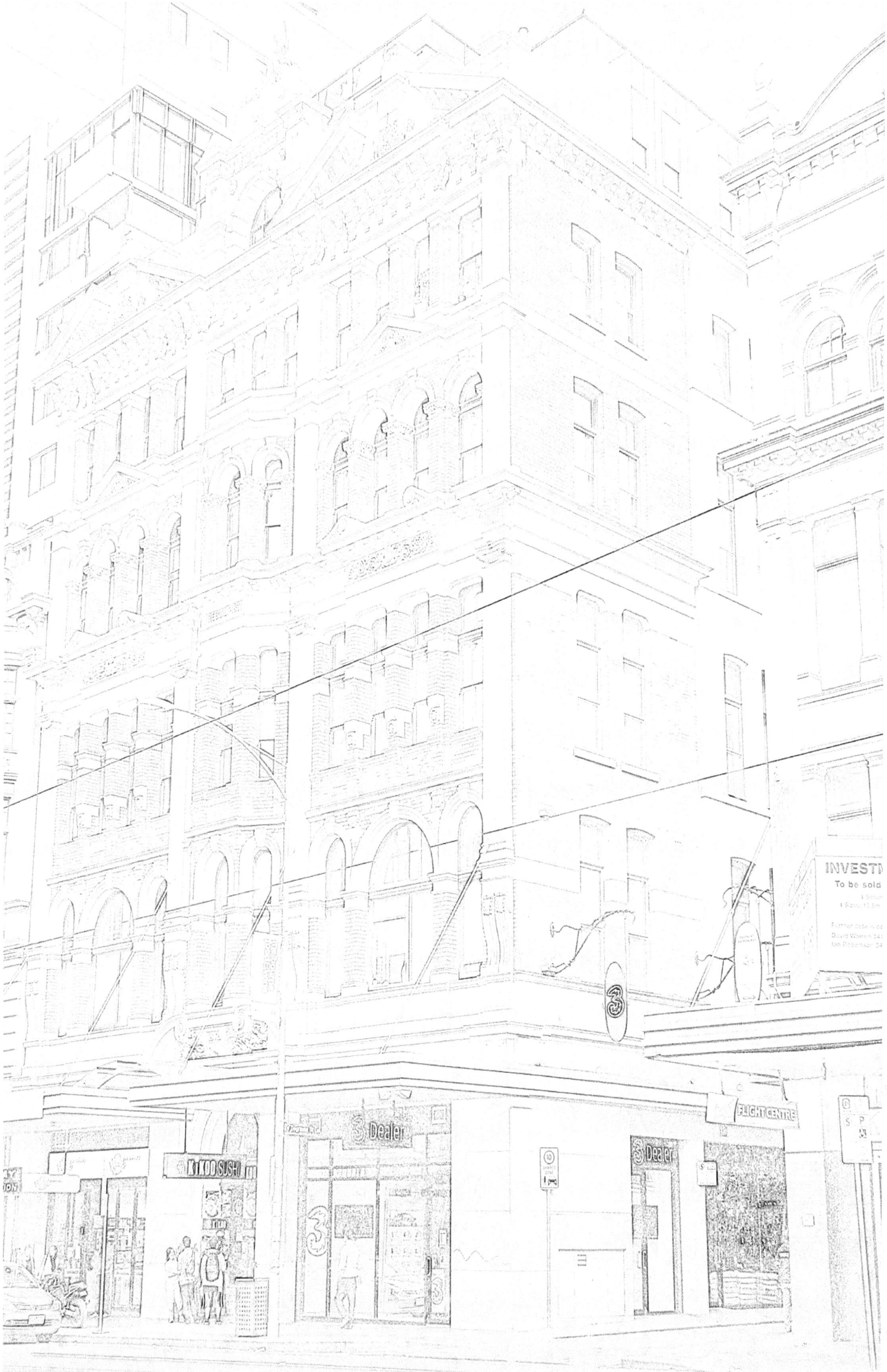
INVESTM
To be sold
3 Dealer
KIKOO SUSHI
FLIGHT CENTRE
3 Dealer

P
KP
172-192 FLINDER
TAXI

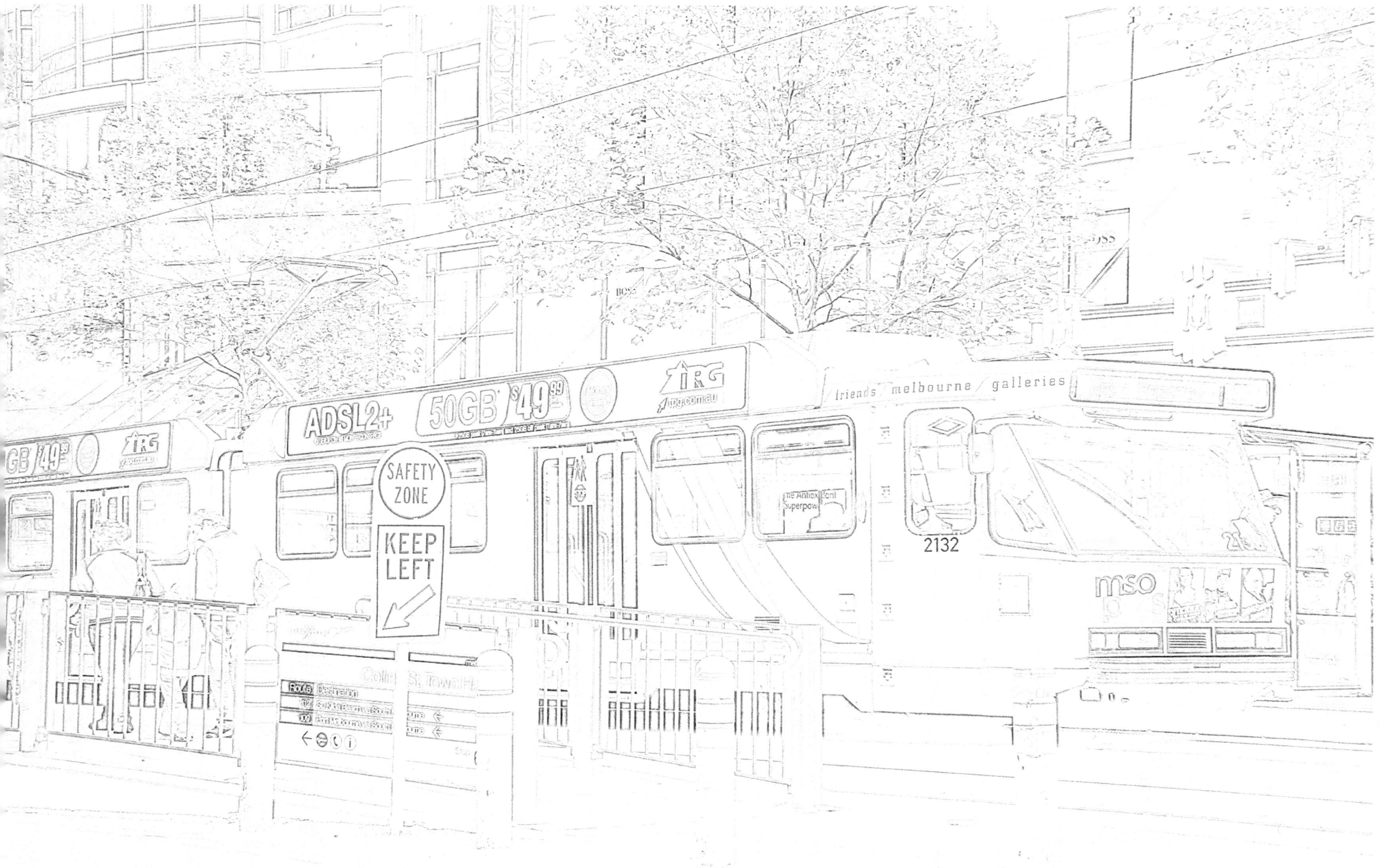
ADSL2+
50GB
$49.99
TPG
tpg.com.au
SAFETY ZONE
KEEP LEFT
friends / melbourne / galleries
2132
mso
BOSS

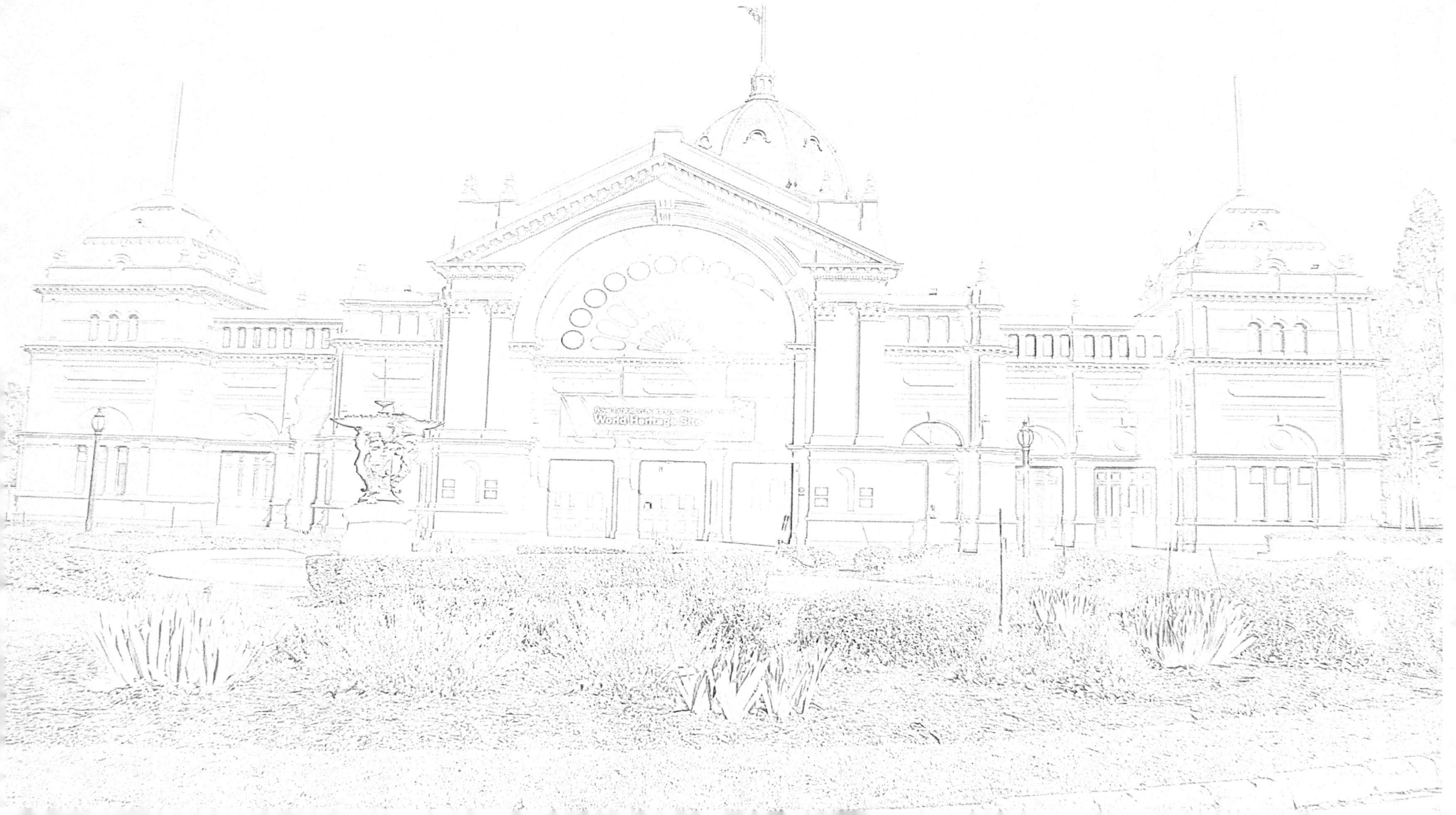
World Heritage

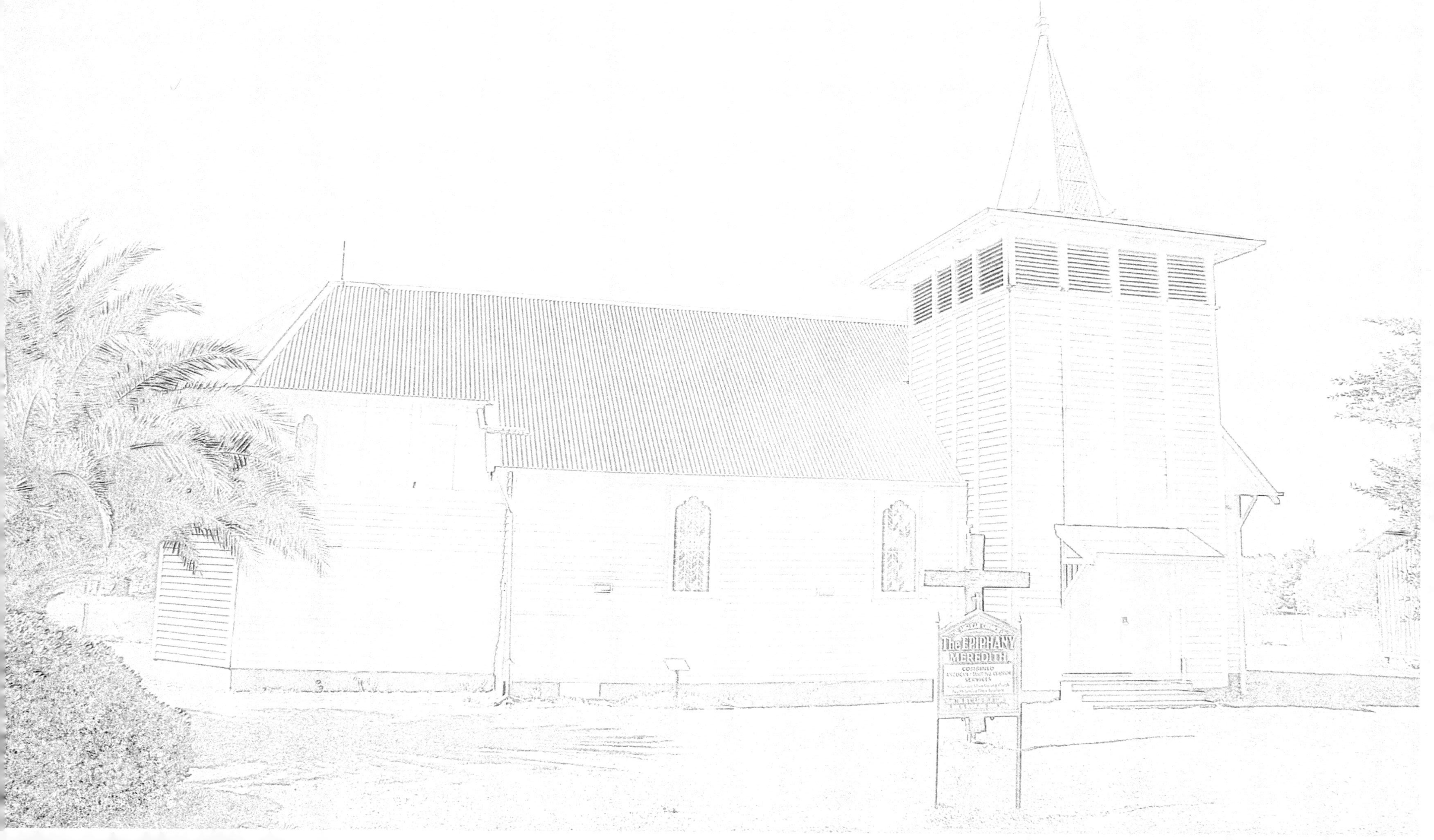
The EPIPHANY
MEREDITH
COMBINED
SERVICES

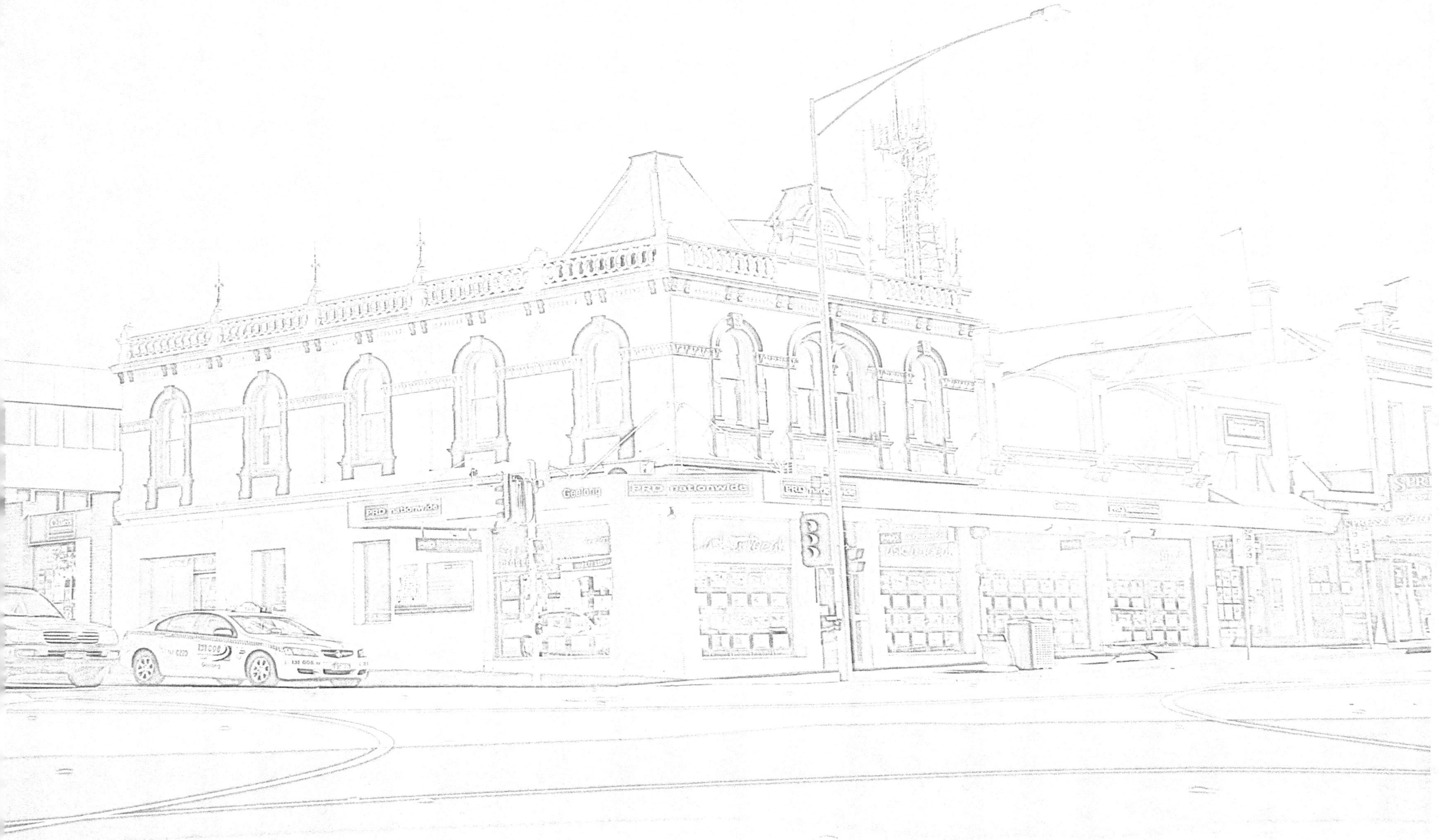
Geelong
PRD nationwide
PRD nationwide
131 008
Geelong

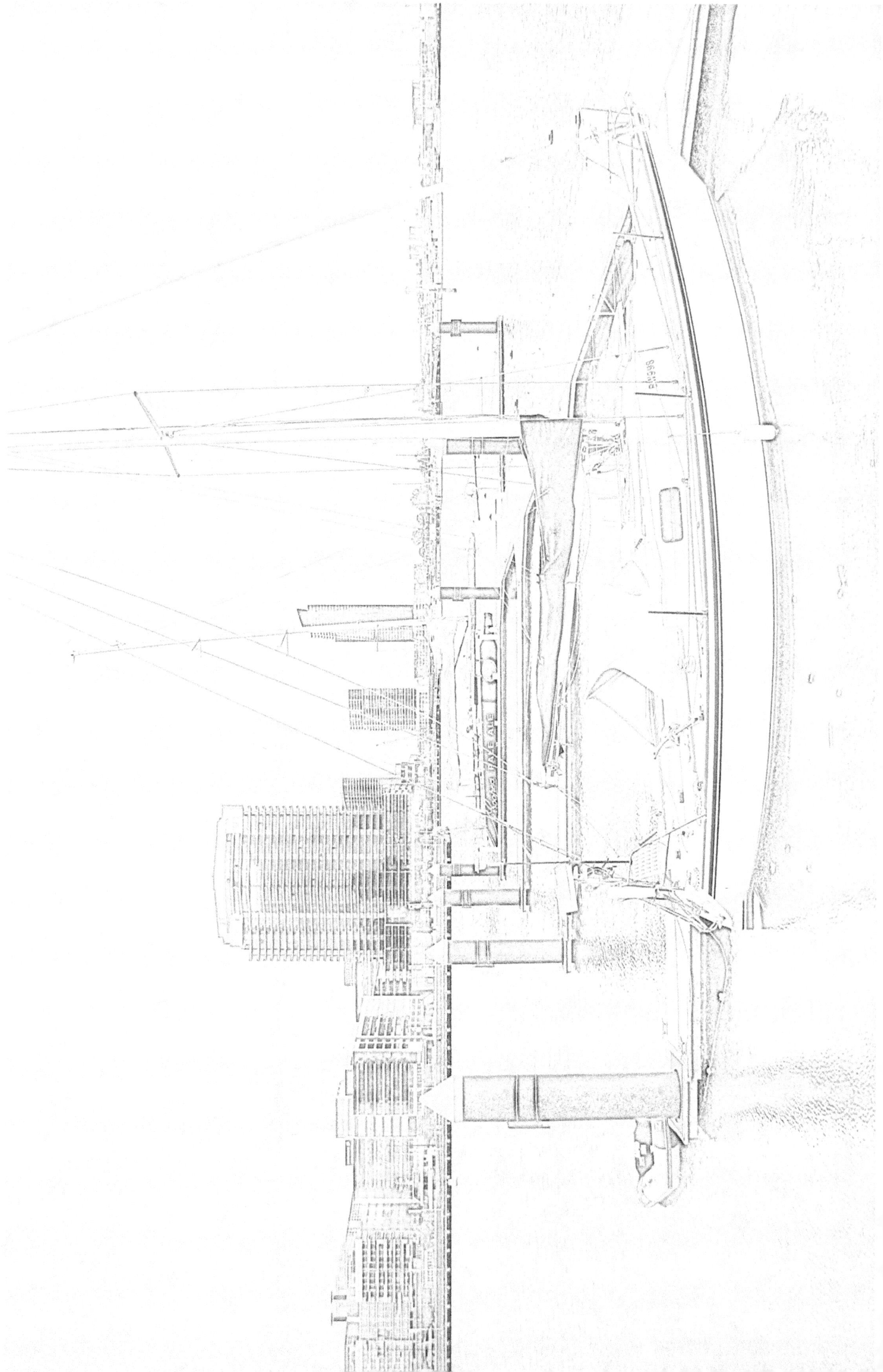

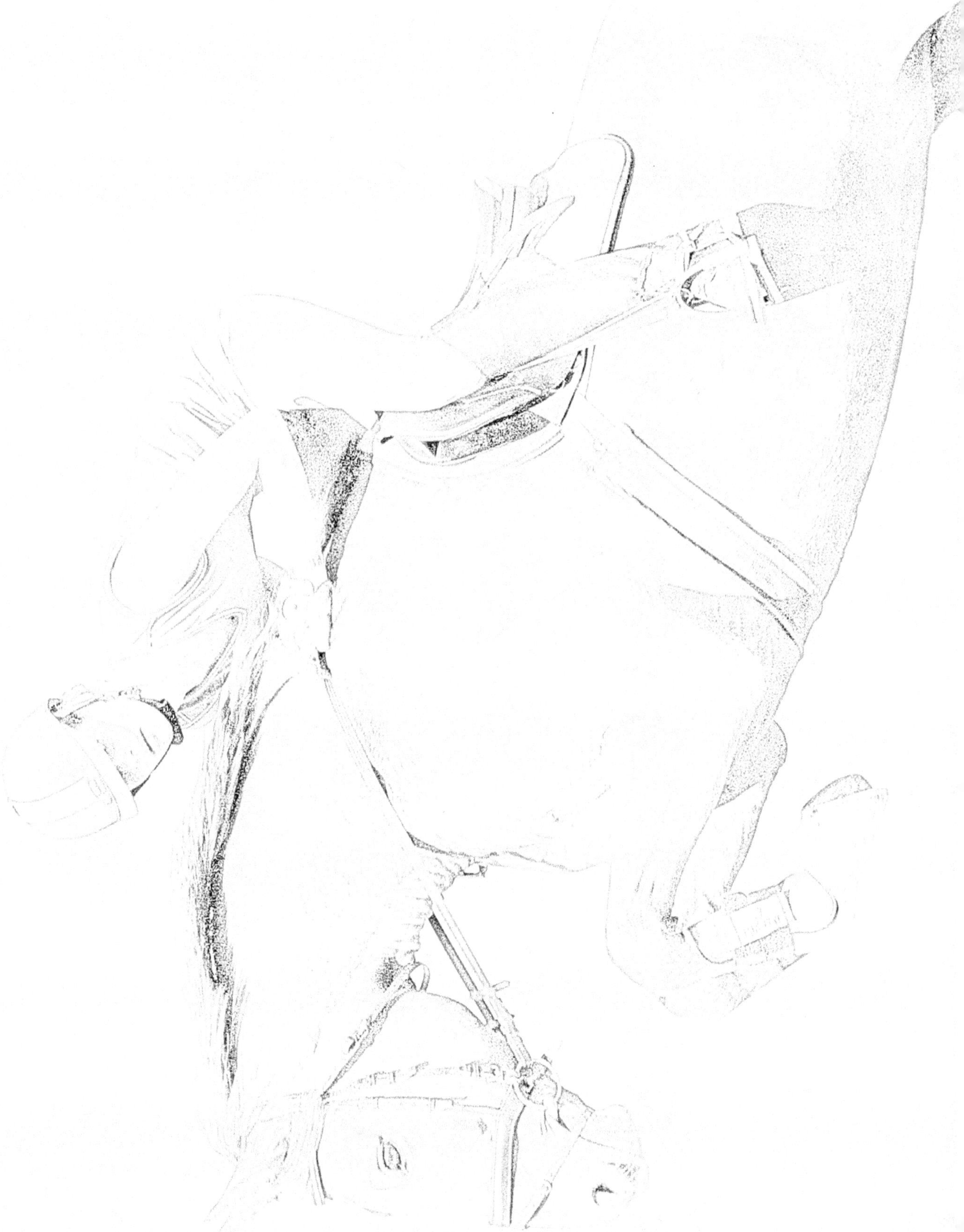

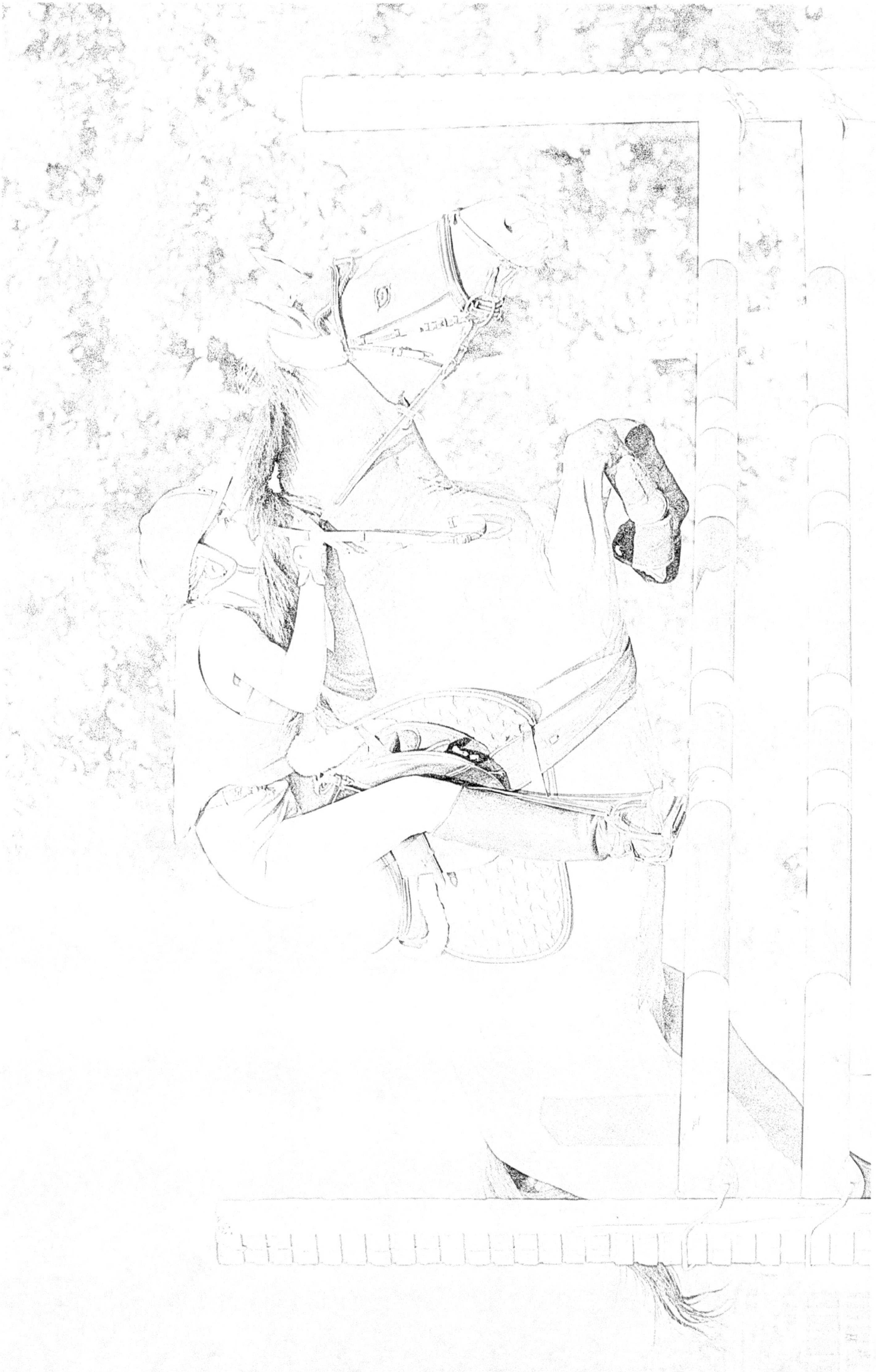

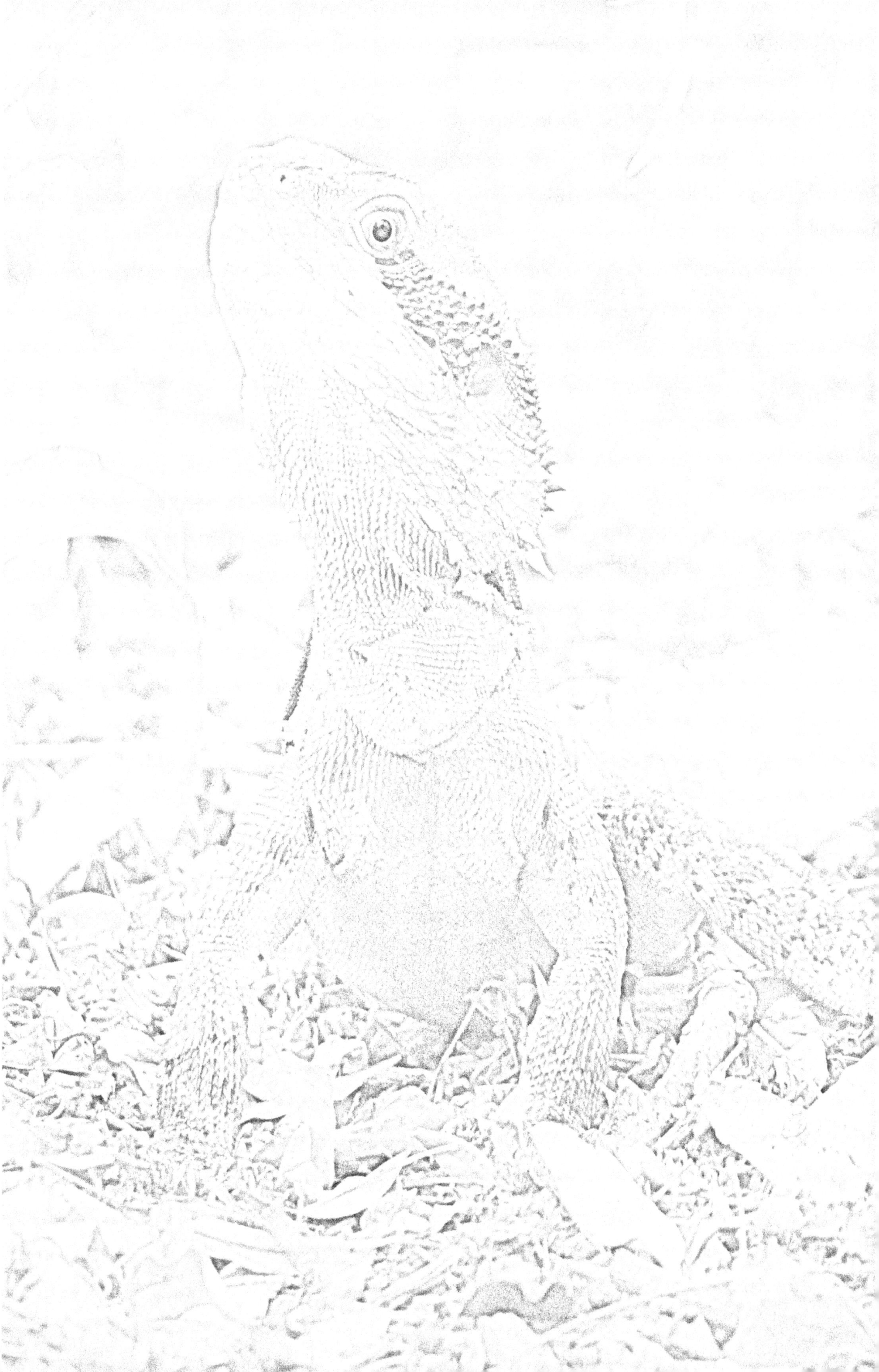

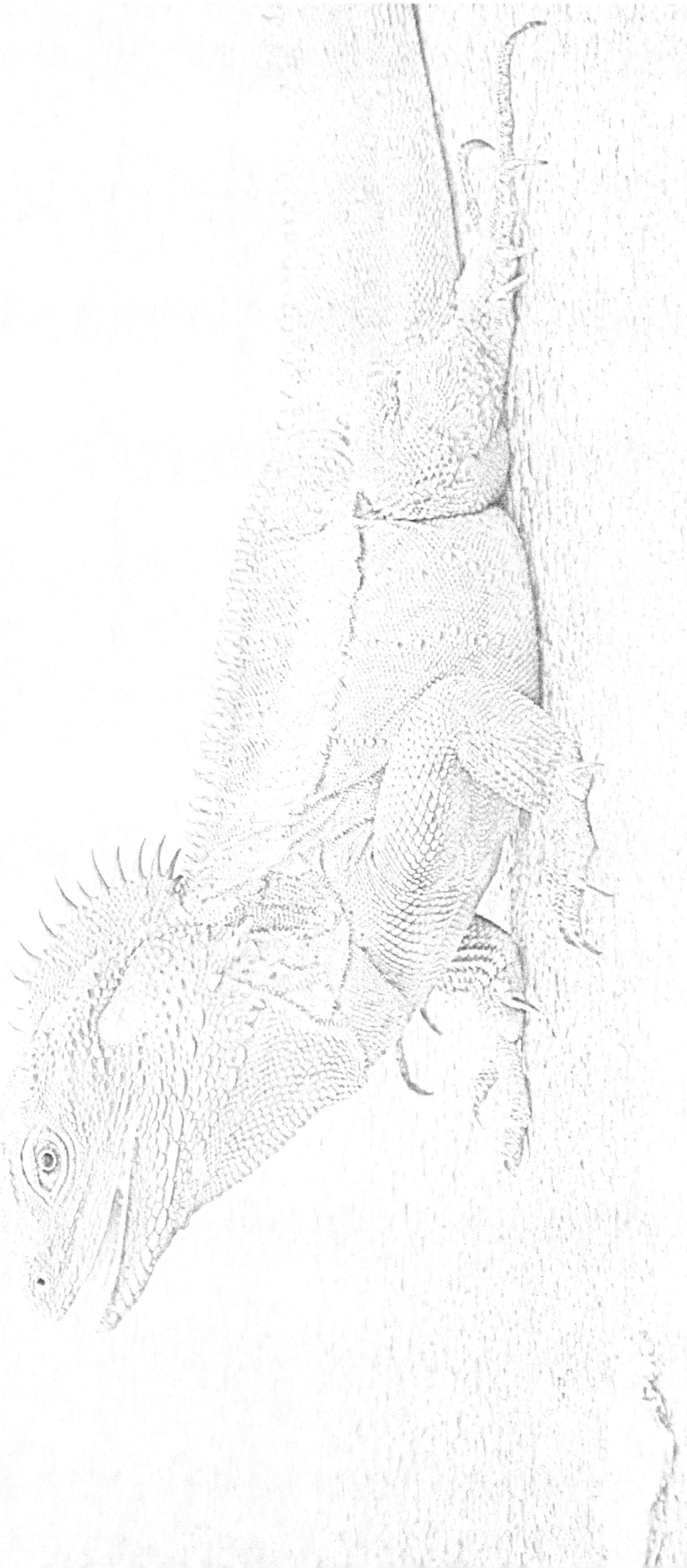

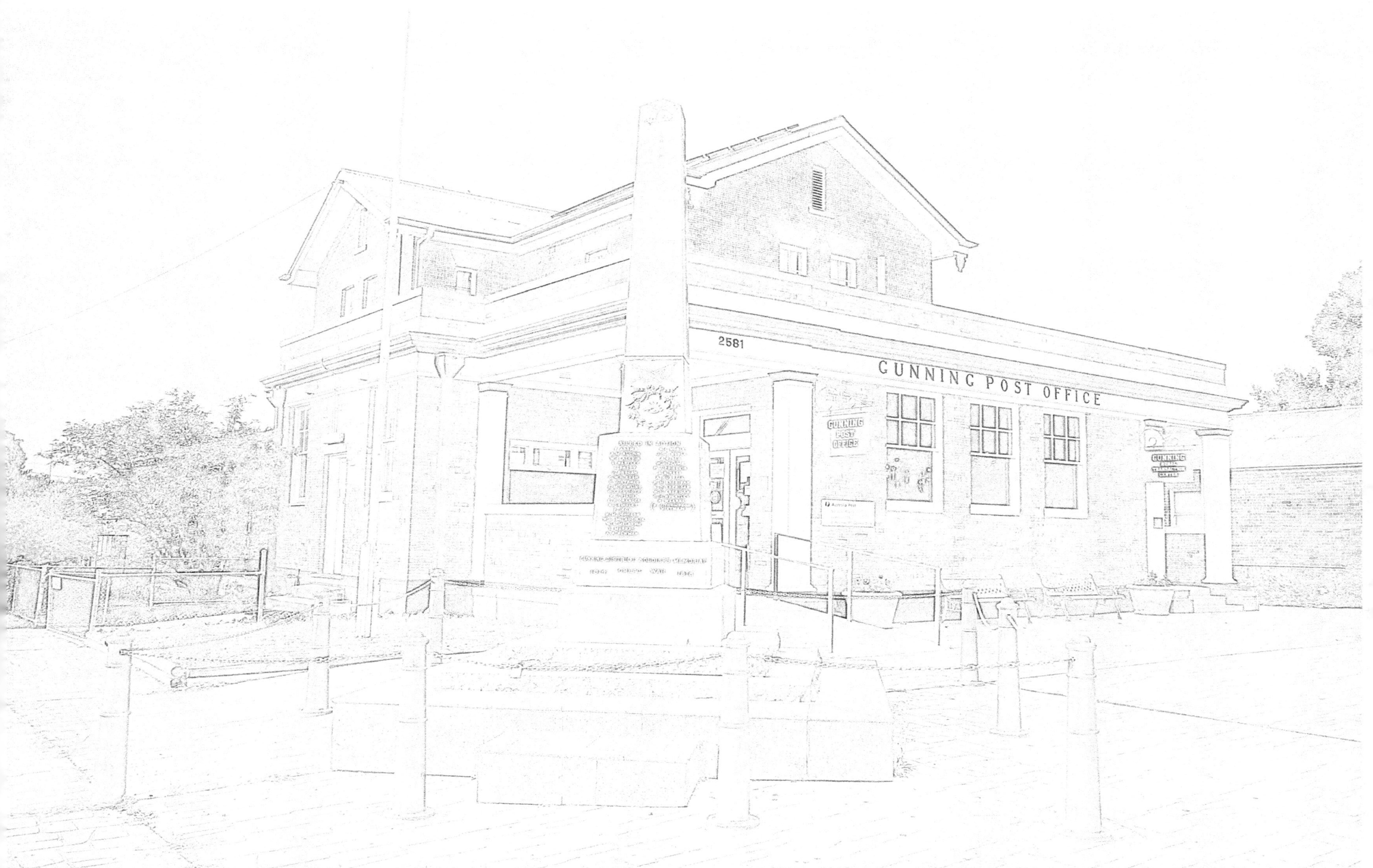

2581
GUNNING POST OFFICE
GUNNING
POST
OFFICE

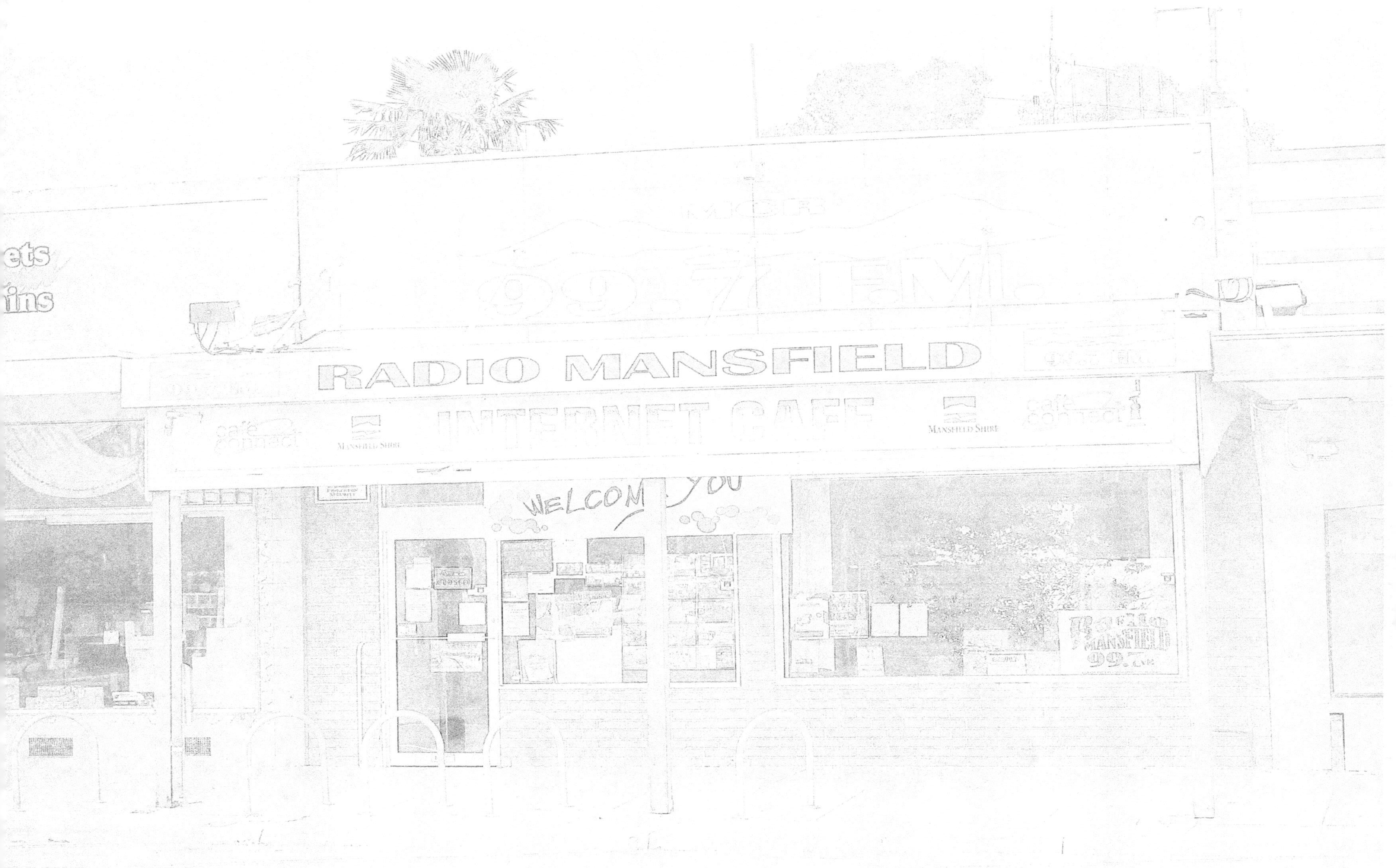

99.7 FM
RADIO MANSFIELD
INTERNET CAFE
cafe connect
MANSFIELD SHIRE
WELCOME YOU
CLOSED
Radio Mansfield 99.7FM
ets
ins

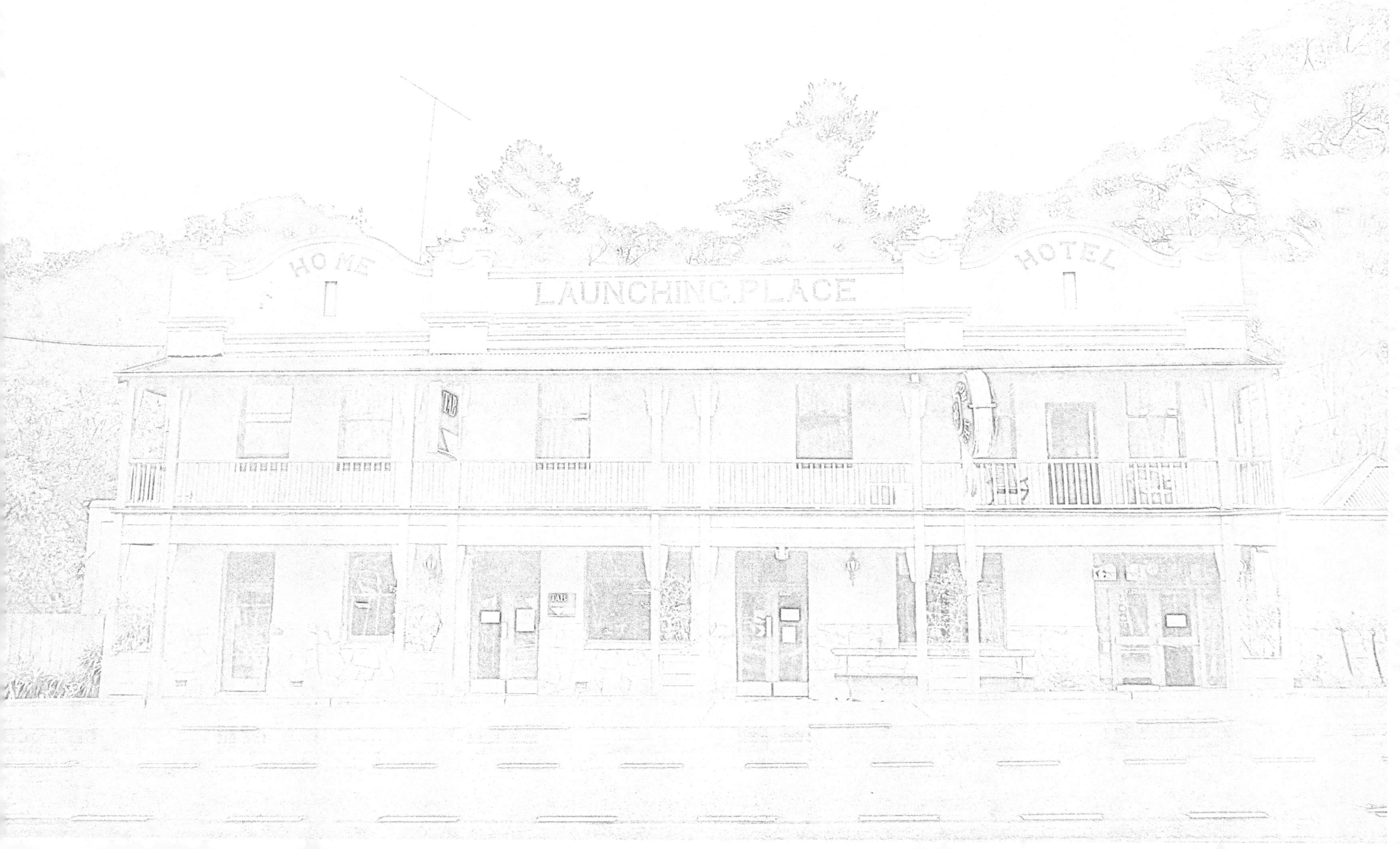
HOME
LAUNCHING PLACE
HOTEL
TAB
TAB

www.ingramcontent.com/pod-product-compliance
Lightning Source LLC
Chambersburg PA
CBHW081050180526
45170CB00005B/1751